Take It to Your Seat Centers

Math

1

Domain	Center	Skill	Page
Numbers and Counting	Count to 120	Sequence numbers within 120	5
	Tens and Ones	Know place values in two-digit numbers	19
	Greater, Less, or Equal?	Compare numbers within 100, using greater than, less than, and equal to symbols	31
	Skip Counting	Count by 2s, 5s, and 10s	47
Operations	Add, Then Subtract	Apply the inverse relationship between addition and subtraction in facts to 10	61
	Jump Up to Add	Add numbers with sums to 20	75
	Jump Back to Subtract	Subtract numbers with differences less than 20	87
Measurement and Data	Measure It	Measure length in nonstandard units	99
	Telling Time	Tell time to the hour and half hour	111
	Make a Graph	Build and read a bar graph	123
Geometry	What Shape Is It?	Identify shapes by the number of sides and corners	135
	Fractional Parts	Divide shapes into two or four equal parts	147

Using the Centers

The 12 centers in this book provide hands-on practice to help students master standards-based mathematics skills. It is important to teach each skill and to model the use of each center before asking students to do the tasks independently. The centers are self-contained and portable. Students can work at a desk, at a table, or on a rug, and they can use the centers as often as needed.

Why Use Centers?

- Centers are a motivating way for students to practice important skills.
- They provide for differentiated instruction.
- They appeal especially to kinesthetic and visual learners.
- They are ready to use whenever instruction or practice in the target skill is indicated.

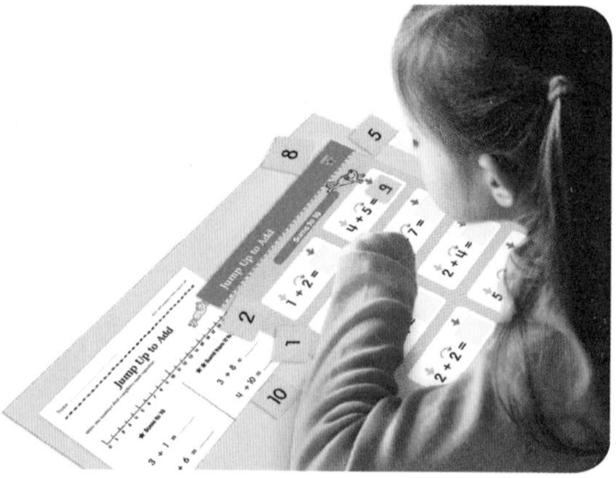

Before Using Centers

You and your students will enjoy using centers more if you think through logistical considerations. Here are a few questions to resolve ahead of time:

- Will students select a center, or will you assign the centers and use them as a skill assessment tool?
- Will there be a specific block of time for centers, or will the centers be used by students throughout the day as they complete other work?
- Where will you place the centers for easy access by students?
- What procedure will students use when they need help with the center tasks?
- Will students use the answer key to check their own work?
- How will you use the center checklist to track completion of the centers?

Introducing the Centers

Use the teacher instructions page and the student directions on the center's cover page to teach or review the skill. Show students the pieces of the center and model how to use them as you read each step of the directions.

Some centers have built-in scaffolding, offering more than one level of practice for the target skill. Carefully review each center beforehand to be sure that you are introducing or assigning the most appropriate level for each student or group.

Recording Progress

Use the center checklist (page 4) to record both the date when a student completes each center and the student's skill level at that point.

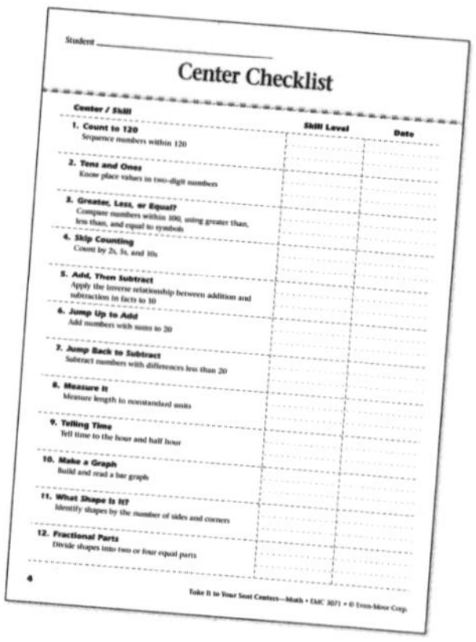

Making the Centers

Included for Each Center

- (A) Student directions/cover page
- (B) Task cards and mat(s)
- (C) Reproducible written practice
- (D) Answer key

Materials Needed

- Folders with inside pockets
- Small envelopes or self-closing plastic bags (for storing task cards)
- Pencils or marking pens (for labeling envelopes)
- Scissors
- Double-sided tape (for attaching the cover page to the front of the folder)
- Laminating equipment

How to Assemble and Store

1. Tape the center's cover page to the front of the folder.
2. Place reproduced written practice pages in the left-hand pocket of the folder.
3. Laminate mats and task cards.
4. Cut apart the task cards and put them in a labeled envelope or self-closing plastic bag. Place the mats and task cards in the right-hand pocket of the folder. If you want the centers to be self-checking, include the answer key in the folder.
5. Store prepared centers in a file box or a crate.

(A)

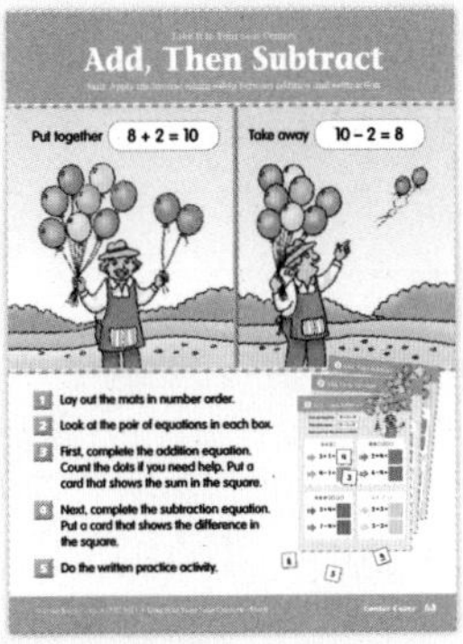

(B)

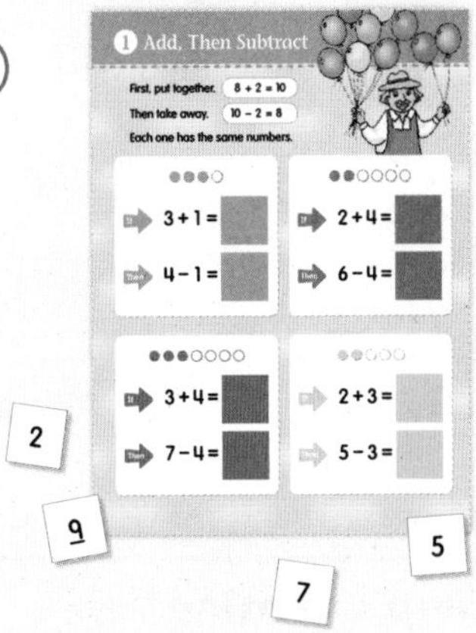

(C)

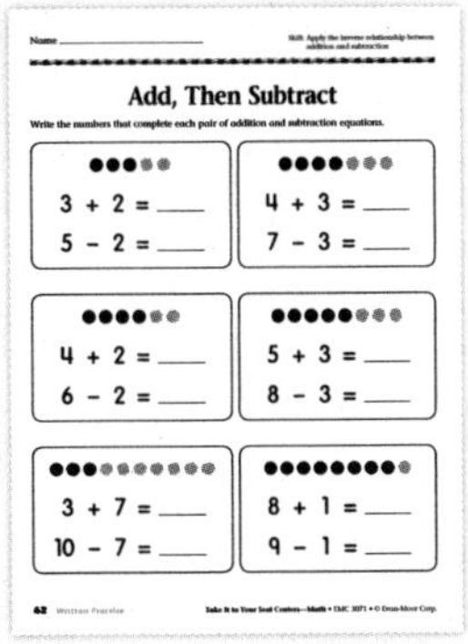

(D) Fold the answer key page in half, as shown. The answers for the mat activity are inside, and the answers for the written practice are on the back.

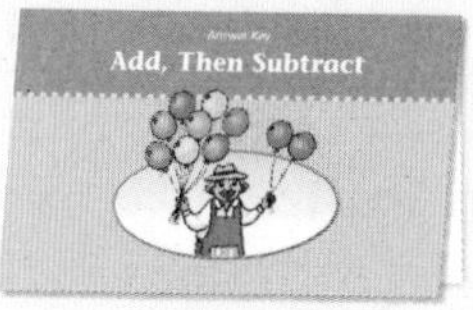

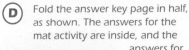

Assembled Center

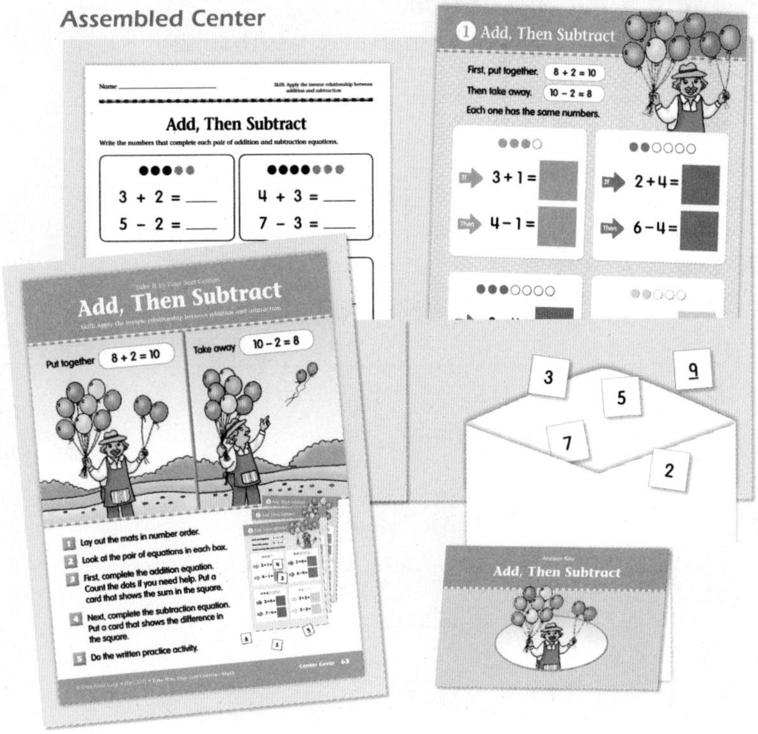

Student ________________________________

Center Checklist

Center / Skill	Skill Level	Date
1. Count to 120 Sequence numbers within 120		
2. Tens and Ones Know place values in two-digit numbers		
3. Greater, Less, or Equal? Compare numbers within 100, using greater than, less than, and equal to symbols		
4. Skip Counting Count by 2s, 5s, and 10s		
5. Add, Then Subtract Apply the inverse relationship between addition and subtraction in facts to 10		
6. Jump Up to Add Add numbers with sums to 20		
7. Jump Back to Subtract Subtract numbers with differences less than 20		
8. Measure It Measure length in nonstandard units		
9. Telling Time Tell time to the hour and half hour		
10. Make a Graph Build and read a bar graph		
11. What Shape Is It? Identify shapes by the number of sides and corners		
12. Fractional Parts Divide shapes into two or four equal parts		

Count to 120

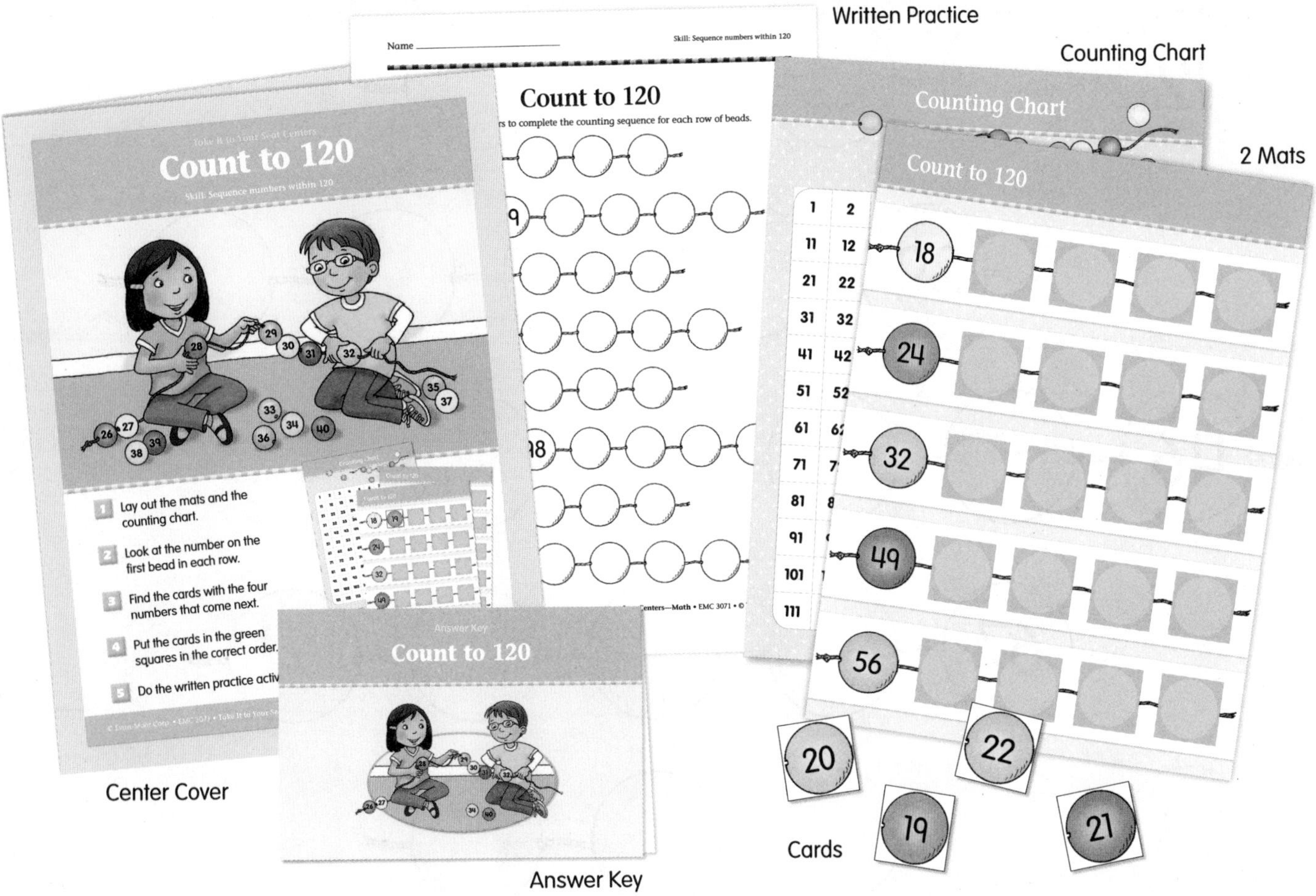

Skill: Sequence numbers within 120

Steps to Follow

1. **Prepare the center.** (See page 3.)
2. **Introduce the center.** State the goal. Say: *You will place number cards in each row on the mats to complete the counting sequence. You may look at the counting chart for help.*
3. **Teach the skill.** Demonstrate how to use the center with individual students or small groups.
4. **Practice the skill.** Have students use the center independently or with a partner.

Contents

Written Practice............... 6
Center Cover.................... 7
Answer Key...................... 9
Counting Chart............. 11
Center Mats 13, 15
Cards 17

Count to 120

Write the missing numbers to complete the counting sequence for each row of beads.

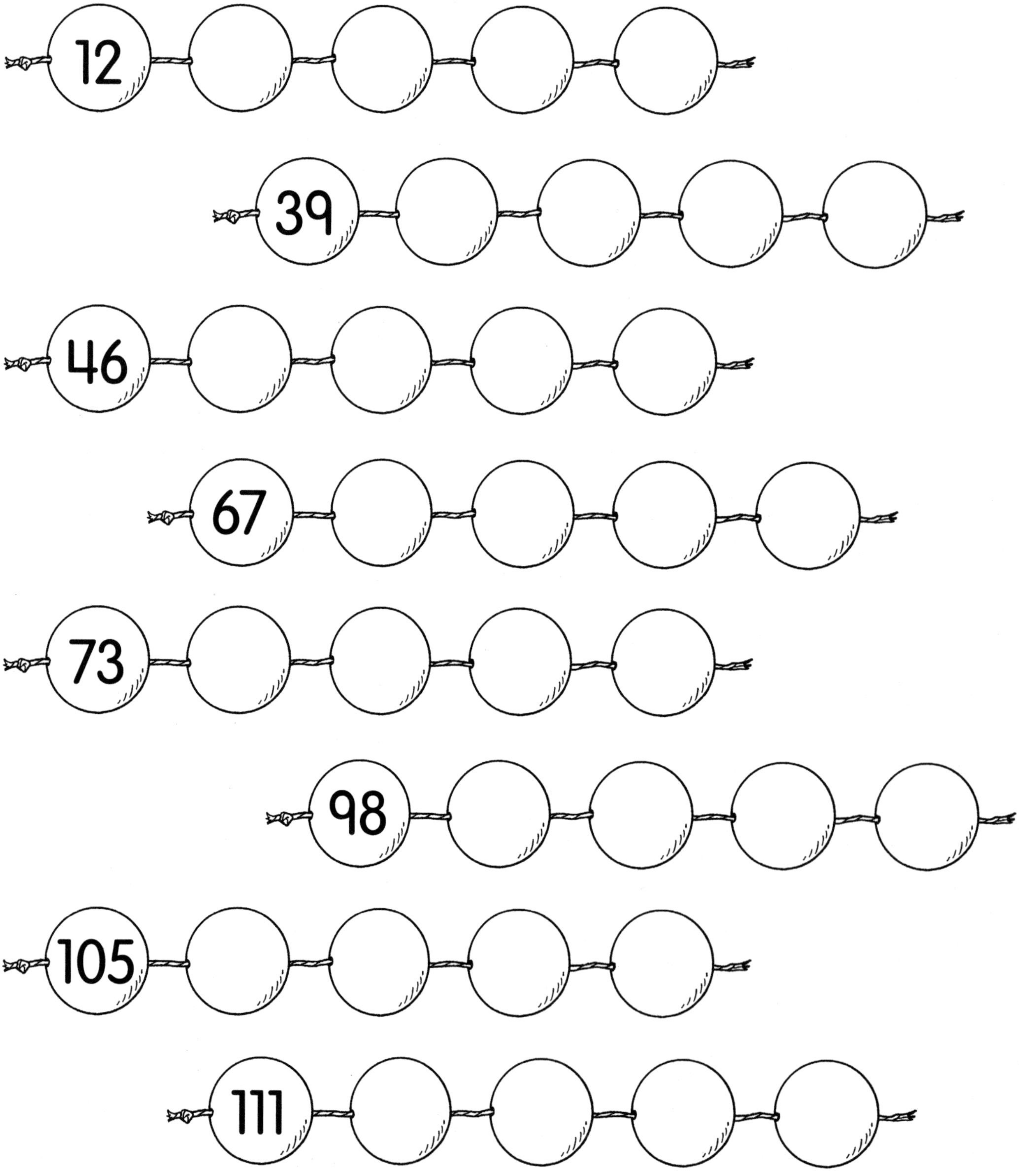

Take It to Your Seat Centers

Count to 120

Skill: Sequence numbers within 120

1. Lay out the mats and the counting chart.
2. Look at the number on the first bead in each row.
3. Find the cards with the four numbers that come next.
4. Put the cards in the green squares in the correct order.
5. Do the written practice activity.

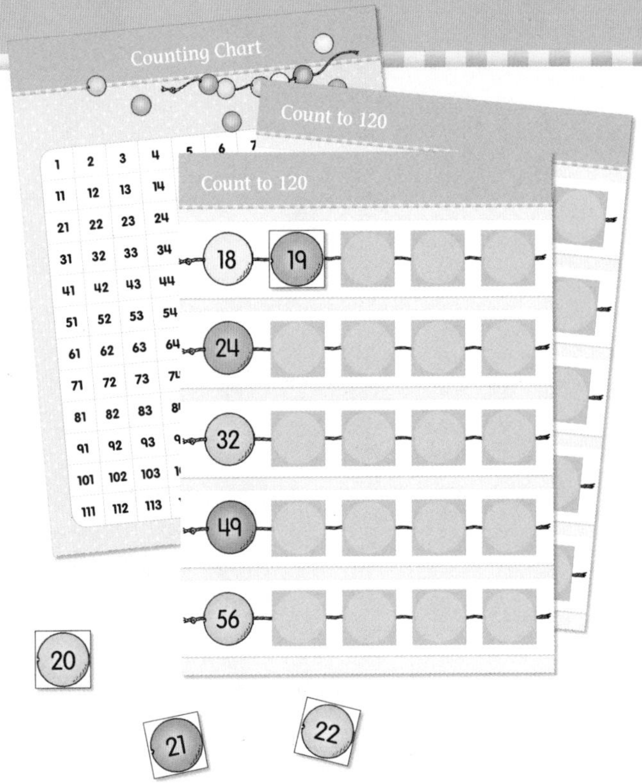

Written Practice

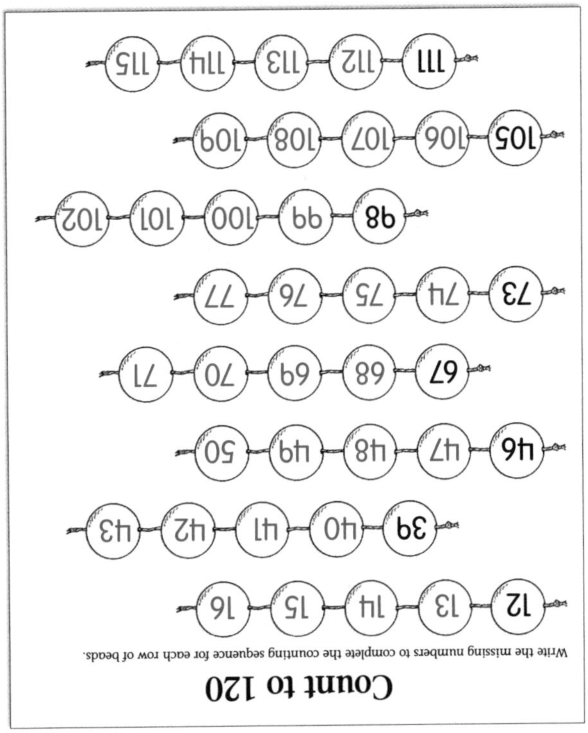
Count to 120

Write the missing numbers to complete the counting sequence for each row of beads.

12 13 14 15 16

39 40 41 42 43

46 47 48 49 50

67 68 69 70 71

73 74 75 76 77

98 99 100 101 102

105 106 107 108 109

111 112 113 114 115

(fold)

Answer Key

Count to 120

Answer Key

Count to 120

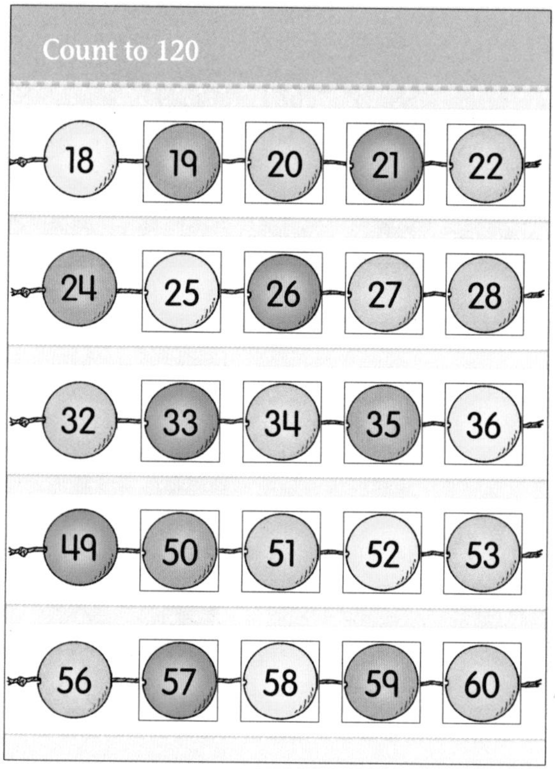

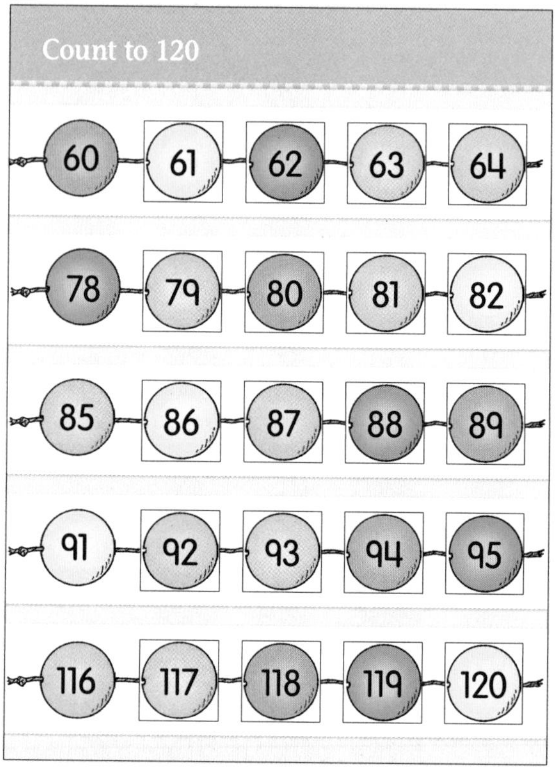

Counting Chart

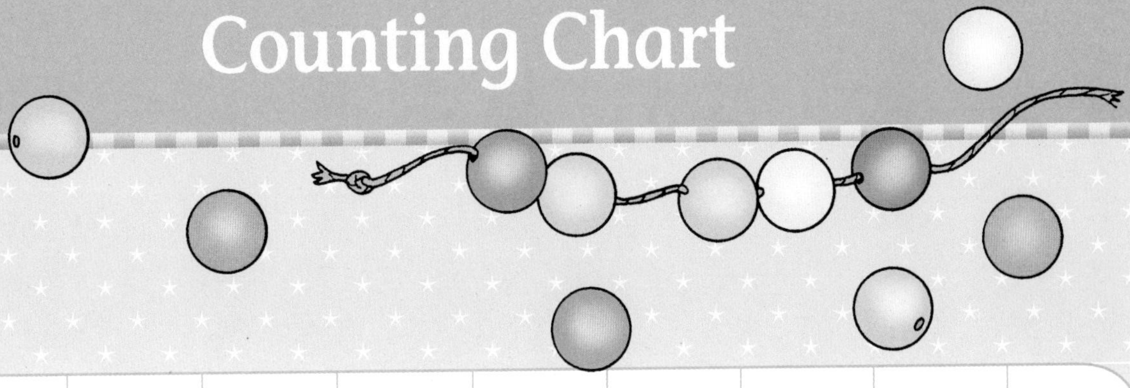

1	2	3	4	5	6	7	8	9	10
11	12	13	14	15	16	17	18	19	20
21	22	23	24	25	26	27	28	29	30
31	32	33	34	35	36	37	38	39	40
41	42	43	44	45	46	47	48	49	50
51	52	53	54	55	56	57	58	59	60
61	62	63	64	65	66	67	68	69	70
71	72	73	74	75	76	77	78	79	80
81	82	83	84	85	86	87	88	89	90
91	92	93	94	95	96	97	98	99	100
101	102	103	104	105	106	107	108	109	110
111	112	113	114	115	116	117	118	119	120

Count to 120

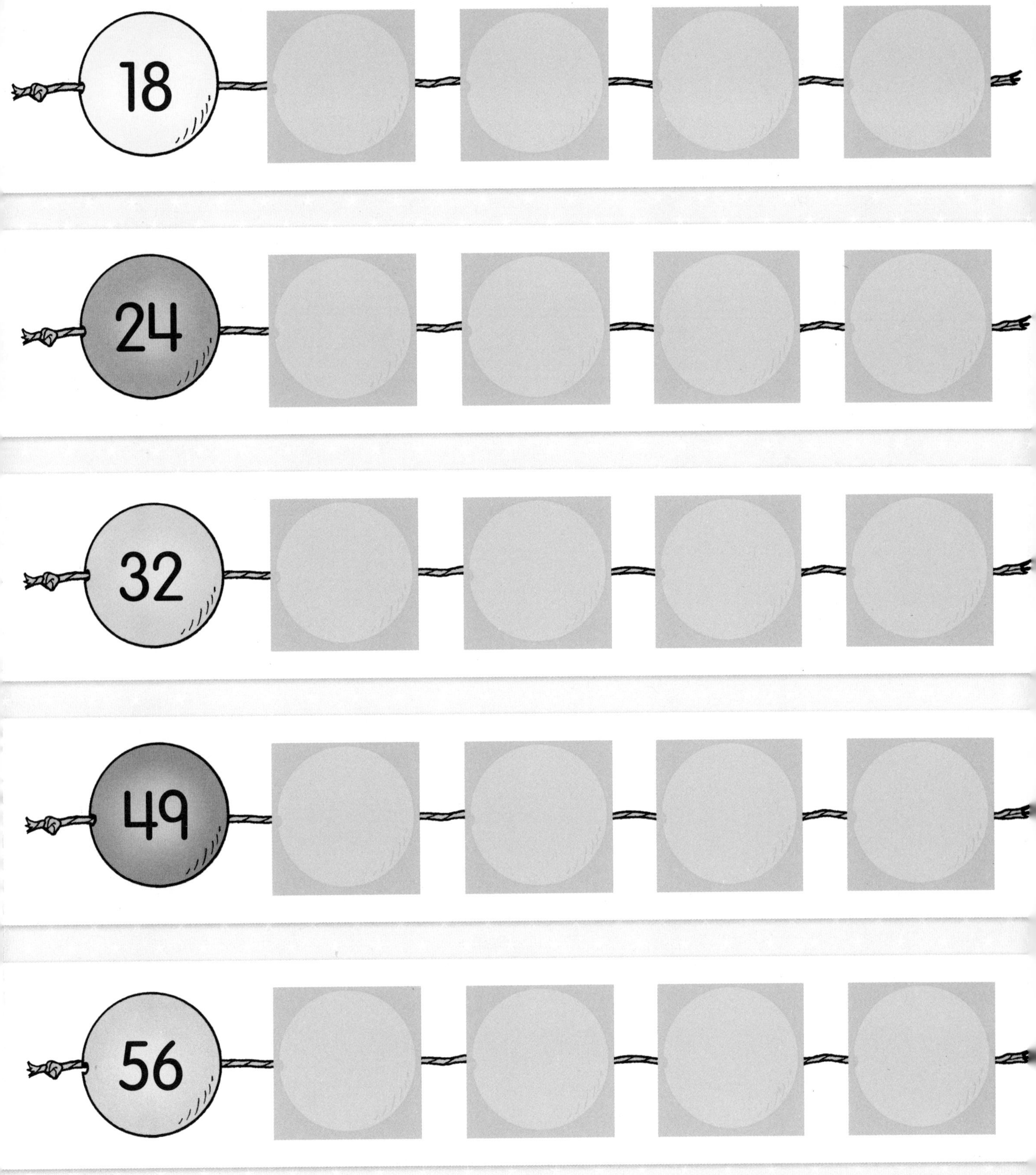

Count to 120

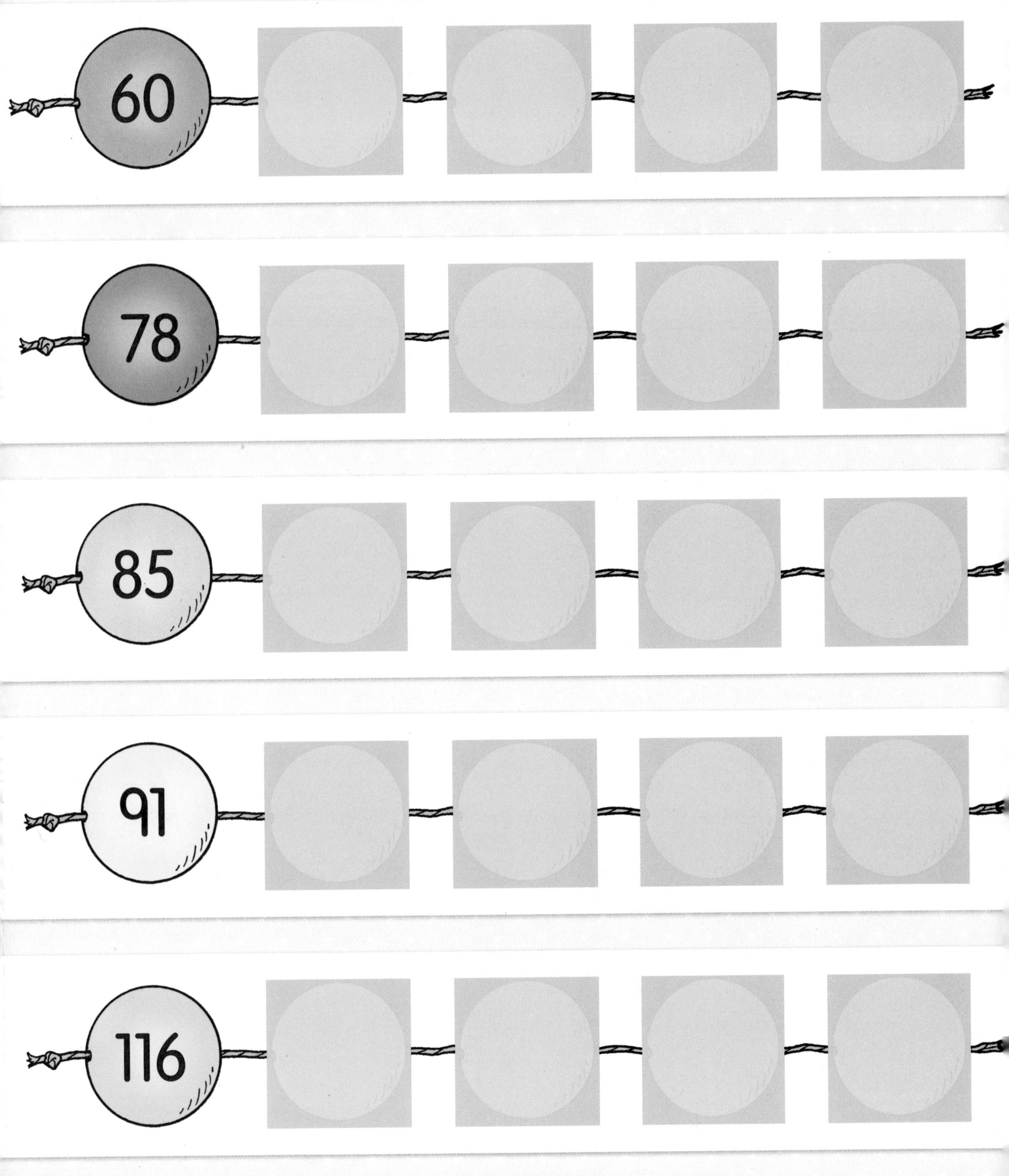

19	20	21	22	25
26	27	28	33	34
35	36	50	51	52
53	57	58	59	60
61	62	63	64	79
80	81	82	86	87
88	89	92	93	94
95	117	118	119	120

Count to 120 EMC 3071 © Evan-Moor Corp.	Count to 120 EMC 3071 © Evan-Moor Corp.	Count to 120 EMC 3071 © Evan-Moor Corp.	Count to 120 EMC 3071 © Evan-Moor Corp.	Count to 120 EMC 3071 © Evan-Moor Corp.
Count to 120 EMC 3071 © Evan-Moor Corp.	Count to 120 EMC 3071 © Evan-Moor Corp.	Count to 120 EMC 3071 © Evan-Moor Corp.	Count to 120 EMC 3071 © Evan-Moor Corp.	Count to 120 EMC 3071 © Evan-Moor Corp.
Count to 120 EMC 3071 © Evan-Moor Corp.	Count to 120 EMC 3071 © Evan-Moor Corp.	Count to 120 EMC 3071 © Evan-Moor Corp.	Count to 120 EMC 3071 © Evan-Moor Corp.	Count to 120 EMC 3071 © Evan-Moor Corp.
Count to 120 EMC 3071 © Evan-Moor Corp.	Count to 120 EMC 3071 © Evan-Moor Corp.	Count to 120 EMC 3071 © Evan-Moor Corp.	Count to 120 EMC 3071 © Evan-Moor Corp.	Count to 120 EMC 3071 © Evan-Moor Corp.
Count to 120 EMC 3071 © Evan-Moor Corp.	Count to 120 EMC 3071 © Evan-Moor Corp.	Count to 120 EMC 3071 © Evan-Moor Corp.	Count to 120 EMC 3071 © Evan-Moor Corp.	Count to 120 EMC 3071 © Evan-Moor Corp.
Count to 120 EMC 3071 © Evan-Moor Corp.	Count to 120 EMC 3071 © Evan-Moor Corp.	Count to 120 EMC 3071 © Evan-Moor Corp.	Count to 120 EMC 3071 © Evan-Moor Corp.	Count to 120 EMC 3071 © Evan-Moor Corp.
Count to 120 EMC 3071 © Evan-Moor Corp.	Count to 120 EMC 3071 © Evan-Moor Corp.	Count to 120 EMC 3071 © Evan-Moor Corp.	Count to 120 EMC 3071 © Evan-Moor Corp.	Count to 120 EMC 3071 © Evan-Moor Corp.
Count to 120 EMC 3071 © Evan-Moor Corp.	Count to 120 EMC 3071 © Evan-Moor Corp.	Count to 120 EMC 3071 © Evan-Moor Corp.	Count to 120 EMC 3071 © Evan-Moor Corp.	Count to 120 EMC 3071 © Evan-Moor Corp.

Tens and Ones

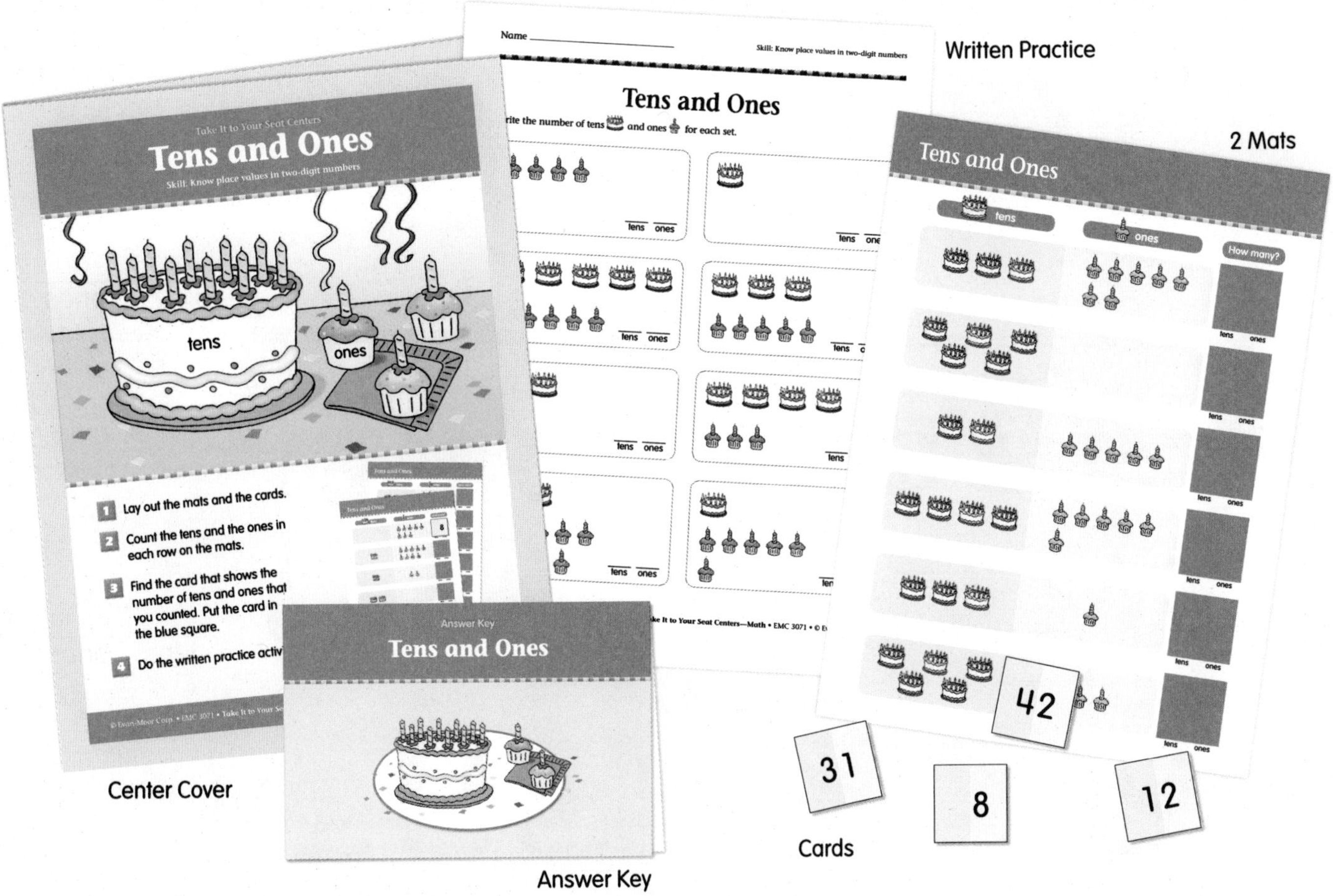

Skill: Know place values in two-digit numbers

Steps to Follow

1. **Prepare the center.** (See page 3.)
2. **Introduce the center.** State the goal. Say: *You will find the correct number card for each row of tens and ones on the mats.*
3. **Teach the skill.** Demonstrate how to use the center with individual students or small groups.
4. **Practice the skill.** Have students use the center independently or with a partner.

Contents

Written Practice............20
Center Cover.................21
Answer Key...................23
Center Mats............25, 27
Cards..........................29

Name ______________________ Skill: Know place values in two-digit numbers

Tens and Ones

Write the number of tens  and ones  for each set.

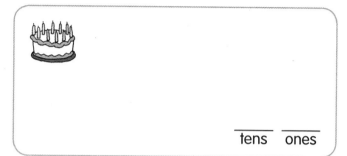

___ tens ___ ones

___ tens ___ ones

___ tens ___ ones

___ tens ___ ones

___ tens ___ ones

___ tens ___ ones

___ tens ___ ones

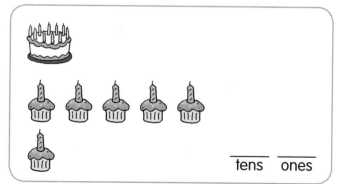

___ tens ___ ones

Take It to Your Seat Centers

Tens and Ones

Skill: Know place values in two-digit numbers

1. Lay out the mats and the cards.
2. Count the tens and the ones in each row on the mats.
3. Find the card that shows the number of tens and ones that you counted. Put the card in the blue square.
4. Do the written practice activity.

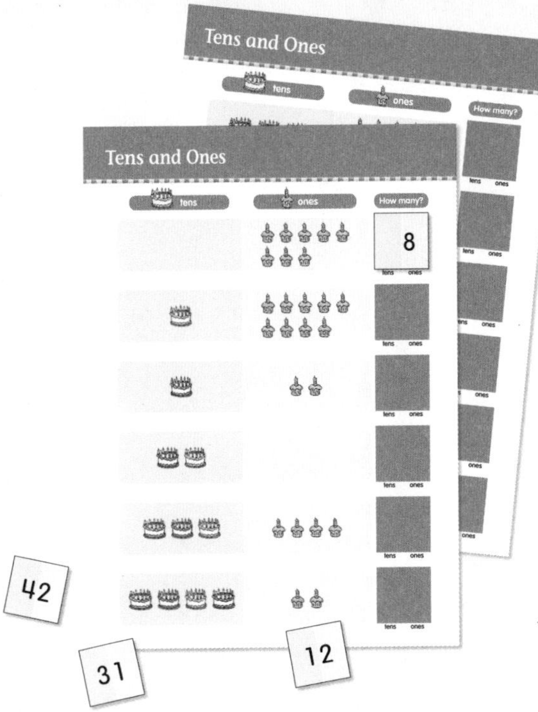

Tens and Ones

Answer Key

(fold)

Written Practice

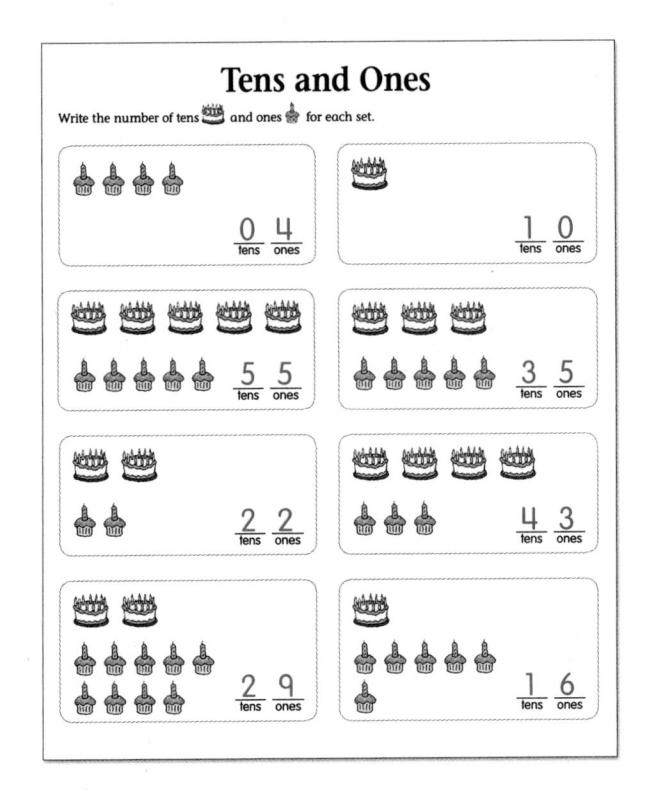

Tens and Ones

Write the number of tens and ones for each set.

0 tens 4 ones	1 tens 0 ones
5 tens 5 ones	3 tens 5 ones
2 tens 2 ones	4 tens 3 ones
2 tens 9 ones	1 tens 6 ones

Answer Key

Tens and Ones

Tens and Ones

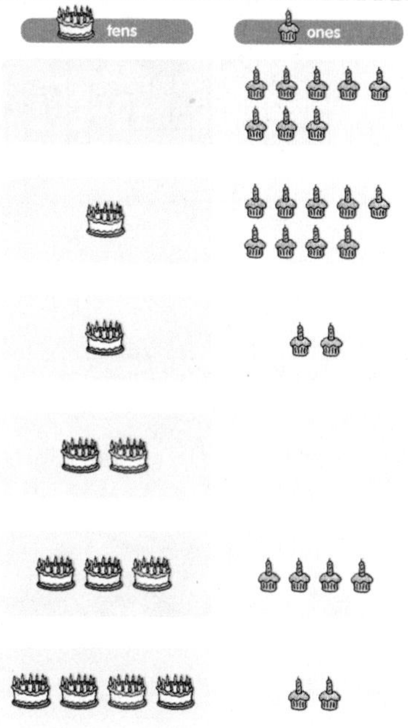

tens	ones	How many?
		8 (tens ones)
		19 (tens ones)
		12 (tens ones)
		20 (tens ones)
		34 (tens ones)
		42 (tens ones)

Tens and Ones

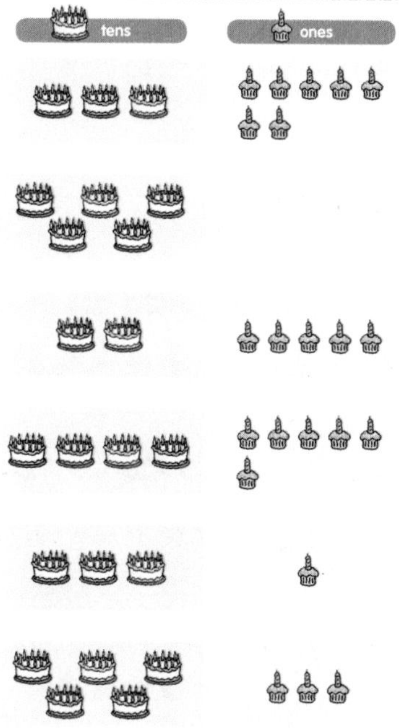

tens	ones	How many?
		37 (tens ones)
		50 (tens ones)
		25 (tens ones)
		46 (tens ones)
		31 (tens ones)
		53 (tens ones)

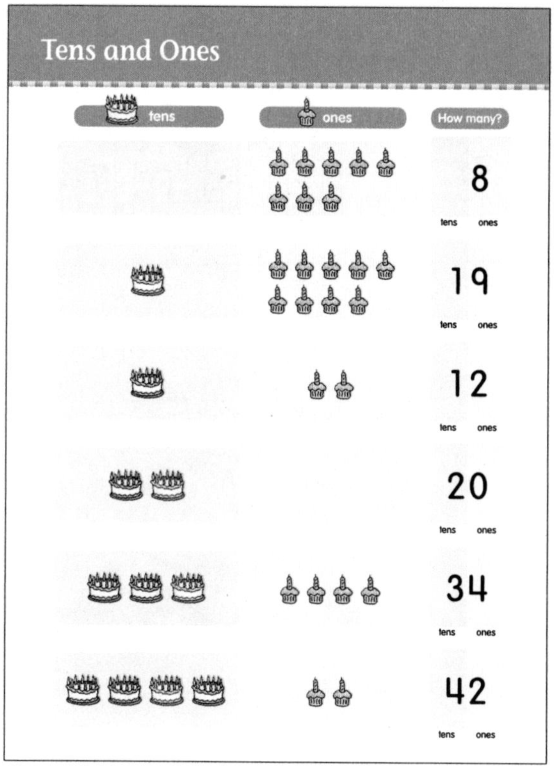

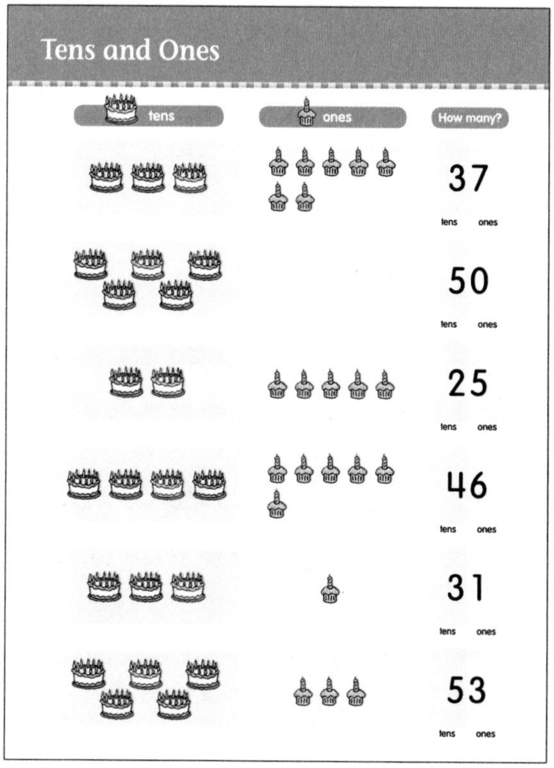

Tens and Ones

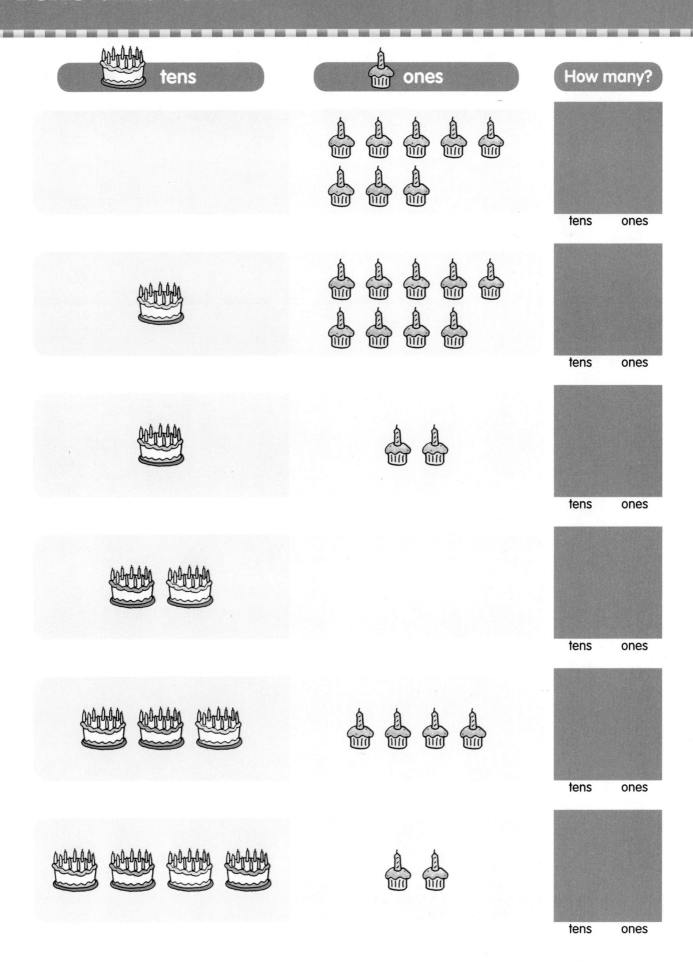

tens	ones	How many?
		tens ones
		tens ones
		tens ones
		tens ones
		tens ones
		tens ones

Tens and Ones

tens | ones | How many?

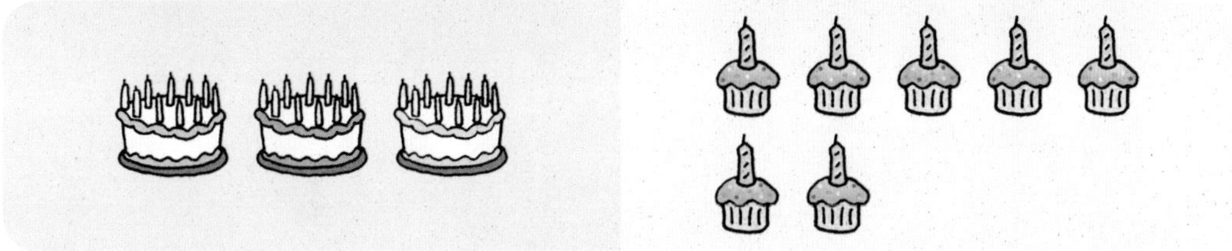

tens ones

tens ones

tens ones

tens ones

tens ones

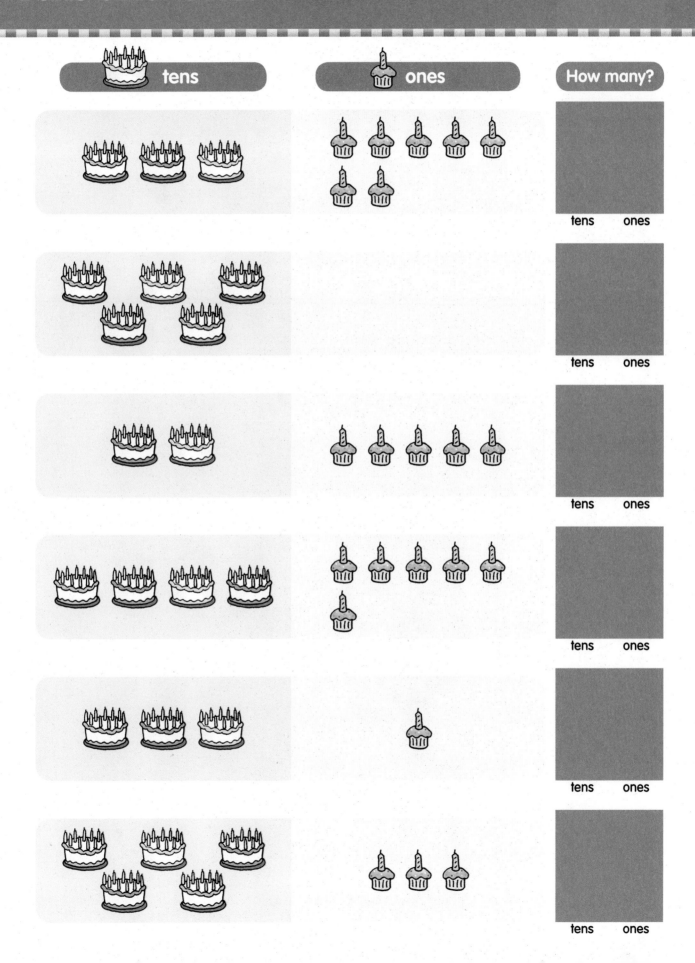

tens ones

8	15	12	34
20	25	31	37
38	42	50	53
19	14	46	5

Tens and Ones EMC 3071 © Evan-Moor Corp.	Tens and Ones EMC 3071 © Evan-Moor Corp.	Tens and Ones EMC 3071 © Evan-Moor Corp.	Tens and Ones EMC 3071 © Evan-Moor Corp.
Tens and Ones EMC 3071 © Evan-Moor Corp.	Tens and Ones EMC 3071 © Evan-Moor Corp.	Tens and Ones EMC 3071 © Evan-Moor Corp.	Tens and Ones EMC 3071 © Evan-Moor Corp.
Tens and Ones EMC 3071 © Evan-Moor Corp.	Tens and Ones EMC 3071 © Evan-Moor Corp.	Tens and Ones EMC 3071 © Evan-Moor Corp.	Tens and Ones EMC 3071 © Evan-Moor Corp.
Tens and Ones EMC 3071 © Evan-Moor Corp.	Tens and Ones EMC 3071 © Evan-Moor Corp.	Tens and Ones EMC 3071 © Evan-Moor Corp.	Tens and Ones EMC 3071 © Evan-Moor Corp.

Greater, Less, or Equal?

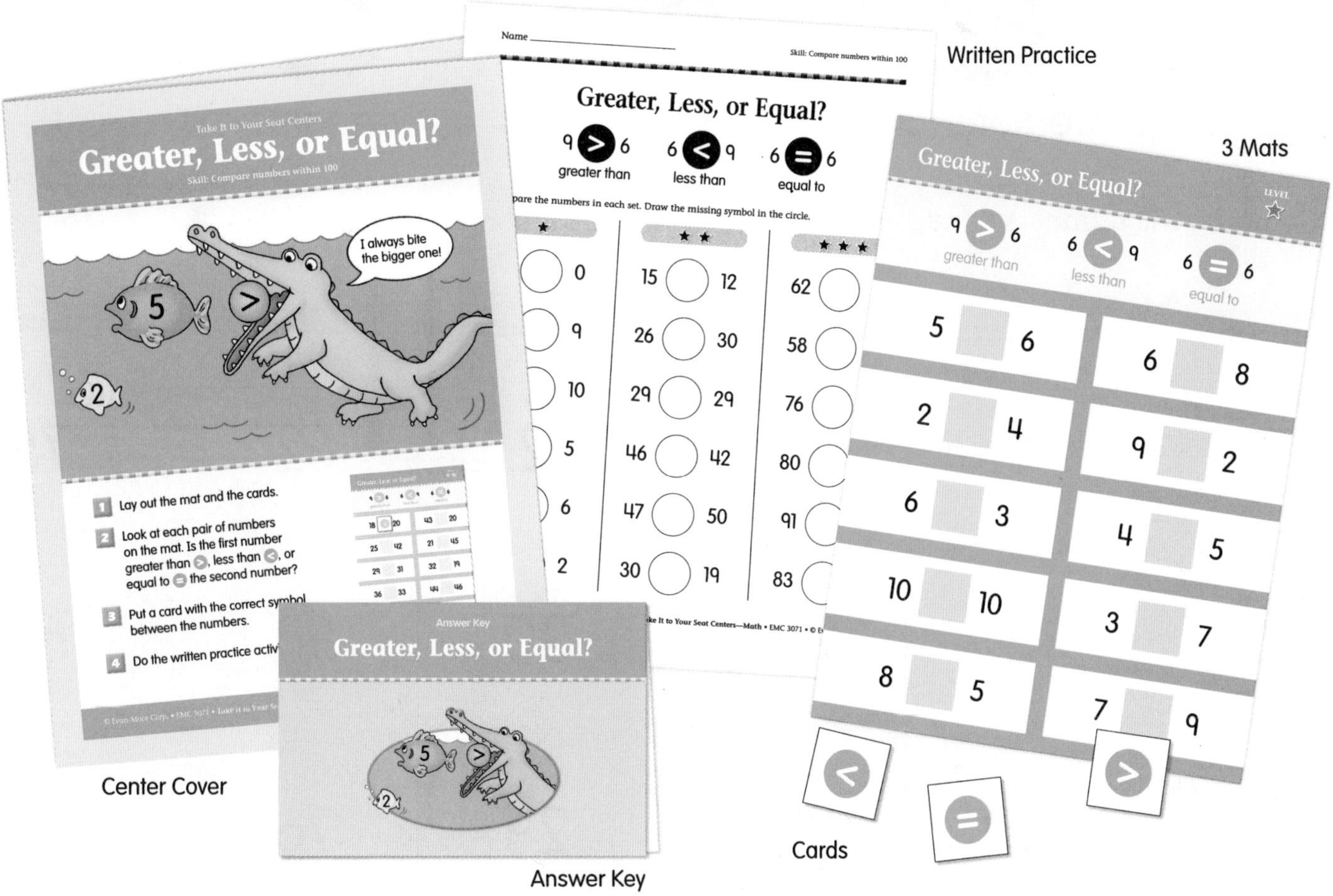

Skill: Compare numbers within 100, using greater than, less than, and equal to symbols

Steps to Follow

1. **Prepare the center.** (See page 3.)
2. **Introduce the center.** State the goal. Say: *You will put a symbol card for greater than, less than, or equal to between each pair of numbers to show how the numbers are related.*
3. **Teach the skill.** Demonstrate how to use the center with individual students or small groups.
4. **Practice the skill.** Have students use the center independently or with a partner.

Contents

Written Practice........... 32
Center Cover................ 33
Answer Key.................. 35
Center Mats
Level 1...................... 37
Level 2...................... 39
Level 3...................... 41
Cards..................... 43, 45

Name ______________________ Skill: Compare numbers within 100

Greater, Less, or Equal?

9 > 6 greater than

6 < 9 less than

6 = 6 equal to

Compare the numbers in each set. Draw the missing symbol in the circle.

★	★★	★★★
1 ◯ 0	15 ◯ 12	62 ◯ 75
3 ◯ 9	26 ◯ 30	58 ◯ 61
8 ◯ 10	29 ◯ 29	76 ◯ 74
5 ◯ 5	46 ◯ 42	80 ◯ 89
9 ◯ 6	47 ◯ 50	91 ◯ 50
7 ◯ 2	30 ◯ 19	83 ◯ 83

Greater, Less, or Equal?

Skill: Compare numbers within 100

1. Lay out the mat and the cards.
2. Look at each pair of numbers on the mat. Is the first number greater than >, less than <, or equal to = the second number?
3. Put a card with the correct symbol between the numbers.
4. Do the written practice activity.

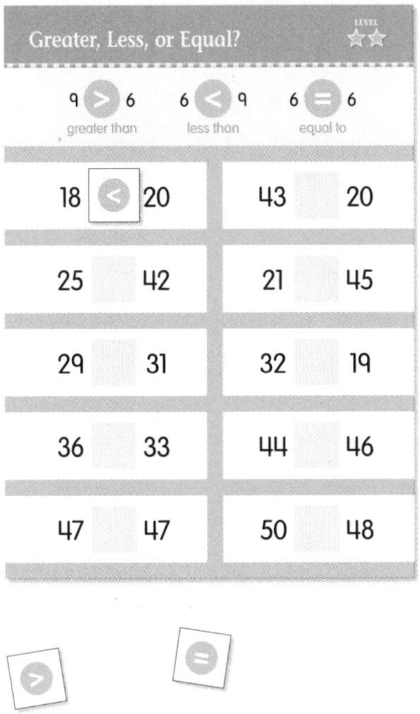
Greater, Less, or Equal?
LEVEL
9 > 6 greater than
6 < 9 less than
6 = 6 equal to
18 < 20
43 20
25 42
21 45
29 31
32 19
36 33
44 46
47 47
50 48
>
=

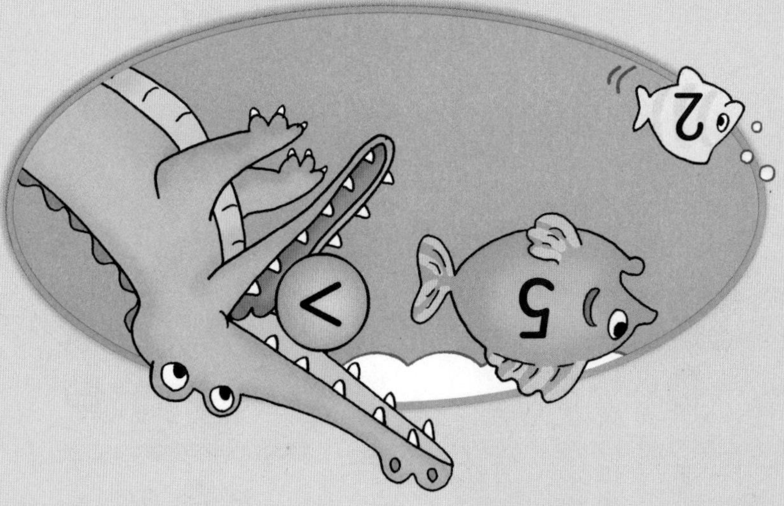

Greater, Less, or Equal?

Answer Key

(fold)

Written Practice

Greater, Less, or Equal?

9 > 6 greater than

6 < 9 less than

6 = 6 equal to

Compare the numbers in each set. Draw the missing symbol in the circle.

★	★ ★	★ ★ ★
1 > 0	15 > 12	62 < 75
3 < 9	26 < 30	58 < 61
8 < 10	29 = 29	76 > 74
5 = 5	46 > 42	80 < 89
9 > 6	47 < 50	91 > 50
7 > 2	30 > 19	83 = 83

Answer Key

Greater, Less, or Equal?

Greater, Less, or Equal? (Level ☆)

9 > 6 greater than | 6 < 9 less than | 6 = 6 equal to

5 < 6	6 < 8
2 < 4	9 > 2
6 > 3	4 < 5
10 = 10	3 < 7
8 > 5	7 < 9

Greater, Less, or Equal? (Level ☆☆)

9 > 6 greater than | 6 < 9 less than | 6 = 6 equal to

18 < 20	43 > 20
25 < 42	21 < 45
29 < 31	32 > 19
36 > 33	44 < 46
47 = 47	50 > 48

Greater, Less, or Equal? (Level ☆☆☆)

9 > 6 greater than | 6 < 9 less than | 6 = 6 equal to

52 < 75	85 < 87
68 > 61	93 < 99
74 = 74	69 < 72
80 > 66	56 < 58
91 > 50	77 > 63

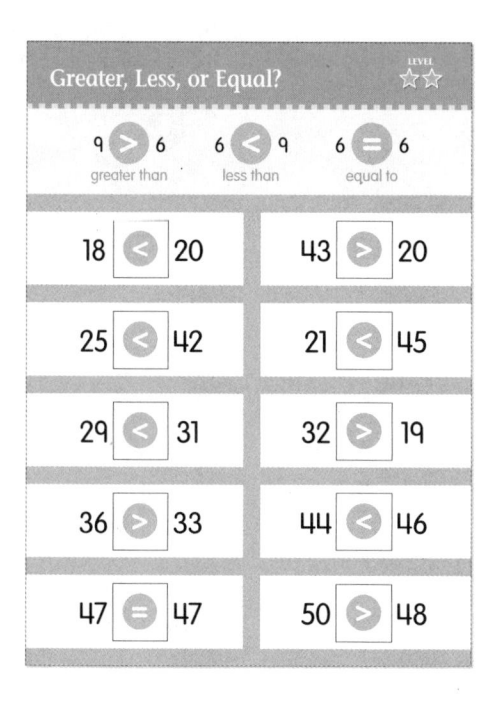

Greater, Less, or Equal?

LEVEL ☆

$9 > 6$ greater than

$6 < 9$ less than

$6 = 6$ equal to

5	☐	6	6	☐	8
2	☐	4	9	☐	2
6	☐	3	4	☐	5
10	☐	10	3	☐	7
8	☐	5	7	☐	9

Greater, Less, or Equal?

LEVEL ☆☆

9 > 6 greater than

6 < 9 less than

6 = 6 equal to

18		20	43		20
25		42	21		45
29		31	32		19
36		33	44		46
47		47	50		48

Greater, Less, or Equal?

LEVEL ★★★

9 > 6 greater than

6 < 9 less than

6 = 6 equal to

52 □ 75	85 □ 87
68 □ 61	93 □ 99
74 □ 74	69 □ 72
80 □ 66	56 □ 58
91 □ 50	77 □ 63

<	<	<	<	<	<	<
<	<	<	<	<	<	<
<	<	<	<	<	<	<
<	<	<	<	<	<	<
=	=	=	=	=	=	=
=	=	=	=	=	=	=
<	<	<	<	<	<	<
<	<	<	<	<	<	<
<	<	<	<	<	<	<

Greater, Less, or Equal? EMC 3071 © Evan-Moor Corp.	Greater, Less, or Equal? EMC 3071 © Evan-Moor Corp.	Greater, Less, or Equal? EMC 3071 © Evan-Moor Corp.	Greater, Less, or Equal? EMC 3071 © Evan-Moor Corp.	Greater, Less, or Equal? EMC 3071 © Evan-Moor Corp.	Greater, Less, or Equal? EMC 3071 © Evan-Moor Corp.	Greater, Less, or Equal? EMC 3071 © Evan-Moor Corp.
Greater, Less, or Equal? EMC 3071 © Evan-Moor Corp.	Greater, Less, or Equal? EMC 3071 © Evan-Moor Corp.	Greater, Less, or Equal? EMC 3071 © Evan-Moor Corp.	Greater, Less, or Equal? EMC 3071 © Evan-Moor Corp.	Greater, Less, or Equal? EMC 3071 © Evan-Moor Corp.	Greater, Less, or Equal? EMC 3071 © Evan-Moor Corp.	Greater, Less, or Equal? EMC 3071 © Evan-Moor Corp.
Greater, Less, or Equal? EMC 3071 © Evan-Moor Corp.	Greater, Less, or Equal? EMC 3071 © Evan-Moor Corp.	Greater, Less, or Equal? EMC 3071 © Evan-Moor Corp.	Greater, Less, or Equal? EMC 3071 © Evan-Moor Corp.	Greater, Less, or Equal? EMC 3071 © Evan-Moor Corp.	Greater, Less, or Equal? EMC 3071 © Evan-Moor Corp.	Greater, Less, or Equal? EMC 3071 © Evan-Moor Corp.
Greater, Less, or Equal? EMC 3071 © Evan-Moor Corp.	Greater, Less, or Equal? EMC 3071 © Evan-Moor Corp.	Greater, Less, or Equal? EMC 3071 © Evan-Moor Corp.	Greater, Less, or Equal? EMC 3071 © Evan-Moor Corp.	Greater, Less, or Equal? EMC 3071 © Evan-Moor Corp.	Greater, Less, or Equal? EMC 3071 © Evan-Moor Corp.	Greater, Less, or Equal? EMC 3071 © Evan-Moor Corp.
Greater, Less, or Equal? EMC 3071 © Evan-Moor Corp.	Greater, Less, or Equal? EMC 3071 © Evan-Moor Corp.	Greater, Less, or Equal? EMC 3071 © Evan-Moor Corp.	Greater, Less, or Equal? EMC 3071 © Evan-Moor Corp.	Greater, Less, or Equal? EMC 3071 © Evan-Moor Corp.	Greater, Less, or Equal? EMC 3071 © Evan-Moor Corp.	Greater, Less, or Equal? EMC 3071 © Evan-Moor Corp.
Greater, Less, or Equal? EMC 3071 © Evan-Moor Corp.	Greater, Less, or Equal? EMC 3071 © Evan-Moor Corp.	Greater, Less, or Equal? EMC 3071 © Evan-Moor Corp.	Greater, Less, or Equal? EMC 3071 © Evan-Moor Corp.	Greater, Less, or Equal? EMC 3071 © Evan-Moor Corp.	Greater, Less, or Equal? EMC 3071 © Evan-Moor Corp.	Greater, Less, or Equal? EMC 3071 © Evan-Moor Corp.
Greater, Less, or Equal? EMC 3071 © Evan-Moor Corp.	Greater, Less, or Equal? EMC 3071 © Evan-Moor Corp.	Greater, Less, or Equal? EMC 3071 © Evan-Moor Corp.	Greater, Less, or Equal? EMC 3071 © Evan-Moor Corp.	Greater, Less, or Equal? EMC 3071 © Evan-Moor Corp.	Greater, Less, or Equal? EMC 3071 © Evan-Moor Corp.	Greater, Less, or Equal? EMC 3071 © Evan-Moor Corp.
Greater, Less, or Equal? EMC 3071 © Evan-Moor Corp.	Greater, Less, or Equal? EMC 3071 © Evan-Moor Corp.	Greater, Less, or Equal? EMC 3071 © Evan-Moor Corp.	Greater, Less, or Equal? EMC 3071 © Evan-Moor Corp.	Greater, Less, or Equal? EMC 3071 © Evan-Moor Corp.	Greater, Less, or Equal? EMC 3071 © Evan-Moor Corp.	Greater, Less, or Equal? EMC 3071 © Evan-Moor Corp.
Greater, Less, or Equal? EMC 3071 © Evan-Moor Corp.	Greater, Less, or Equal? EMC 3071 © Evan-Moor Corp.	Greater, Less, or Equal? EMC 3071 © Evan-Moor Corp.	Greater, Less, or Equal? EMC 3071 © Evan-Moor Corp.	Greater, Less, or Equal? EMC 3071 © Evan-Moor Corp.	Greater, Less, or Equal? EMC 3071 © Evan-Moor Corp.	Greater, Less, or Equal? EMC 3071 © Evan-Moor Corp.

<	<	<	<	<	<	<
<	<	<	<	<	<	<
<	<	<	<	<	<	<
<	<	<	<	<	<	<
=	=	=	=	=	=	=
=	=	=	=	=	=	=
=	=	=	=	=	=	=
=	=	=	=	=	=	=
<	<	<	<	<	<	<

Greater, Less, or Equal? EMC 3071 © Evan-Moor Corp.	Greater, Less, or Equal? EMC 3071 © Evan-Moor Corp.	Greater, Less, or Equal? EMC 3071 © Evan-Moor Corp.	Greater, Less, or Equal? EMC 3071 © Evan-Moor Corp.	Greater, Less, or Equal? EMC 3071 © Evan-Moor Corp.	Greater, Less, or Equal? EMC 3071 © Evan-Moor Corp.	Greater, Less, or Equal? EMC 3071 © Evan-Moor Corp.
Greater, Less, or Equal? EMC 3071 © Evan-Moor Corp.	Greater, Less, or Equal? EMC 3071 © Evan-Moor Corp.	Greater, Less, or Equal? EMC 3071 © Evan-Moor Corp.	Greater, Less, or Equal? EMC 3071 © Evan-Moor Corp.	Greater, Less, or Equal? EMC 3071 © Evan-Moor Corp.	Greater, Less, or Equal? EMC 3071 © Evan-Moor Corp.	Greater, Less, or Equal? EMC 3071 © Evan-Moor Corp.
Greater, Less, or Equal? EMC 3071 © Evan-Moor Corp.	Greater, Less, or Equal? EMC 3071 © Evan-Moor Corp.	Greater, Less, or Equal? EMC 3071 © Evan-Moor Corp.	Greater, Less, or Equal? EMC 3071 © Evan-Moor Corp.	Greater, Less, or Equal? EMC 3071 © Evan-Moor Corp.	Greater, Less, or Equal? EMC 3071 © Evan-Moor Corp.	Greater, Less, or Equal? EMC 3071 © Evan-Moor Corp.
Greater, Less, or Equal? EMC 3071 © Evan-Moor Corp.	Greater, Less, or Equal? EMC 3071 © Evan-Moor Corp.	Greater, Less, or Equal? EMC 3071 © Evan-Moor Corp.	Greater, Less, or Equal? EMC 3071 © Evan-Moor Corp.	Greater, Less, or Equal? EMC 3071 © Evan-Moor Corp.	Greater, Less, or Equal? EMC 3071 © Evan-Moor Corp.	Greater, Less, or Equal? EMC 3071 © Evan-Moor Corp.
Greater, Less, or Equal? EMC 3071 © Evan-Moor Corp.	Greater, Less, or Equal? EMC 3071 © Evan-Moor Corp.	Greater, Less, or Equal? EMC 3071 © Evan-Moor Corp.	Greater, Less, or Equal? EMC 3071 © Evan-Moor Corp.	Greater, Less, or Equal? EMC 3071 © Evan-Moor Corp.	Greater, Less, or Equal? EMC 3071 © Evan-Moor Corp.	Greater, Less, or Equal? EMC 3071 © Evan-Moor Corp.
Greater, Less, or Equal? EMC 3071 © Evan-Moor Corp.	Greater, Less, or Equal? EMC 3071 © Evan-Moor Corp.	Greater, Less, or Equal? EMC 3071 © Evan-Moor Corp.	Greater, Less, or Equal? EMC 3071 © Evan-Moor Corp.	Greater, Less, or Equal? EMC 3071 © Evan-Moor Corp.	Greater, Less, or Equal? EMC 3071 © Evan-Moor Corp.	Greater, Less, or Equal? EMC 3071 © Evan-Moor Corp.
Greater, Less, or Equal? EMC 3071 © Evan-Moor Corp.	Greater, Less, or Equal? EMC 3071 © Evan-Moor Corp.	Greater, Less, or Equal? EMC 3071 © Evan-Moor Corp.	Greater, Less, or Equal? EMC 3071 © Evan-Moor Corp.	Greater, Less, or Equal? EMC 3071 © Evan-Moor Corp.	Greater, Less, or Equal? EMC 3071 © Evan-Moor Corp.	Greater, Less, or Equal? EMC 3071 © Evan-Moor Corp.
Greater, Less, or Equal? EMC 3071 © Evan-Moor Corp.	Greater, Less, or Equal? EMC 3071 © Evan-Moor Corp.	Greater, Less, or Equal? EMC 3071 © Evan-Moor Corp.	Greater, Less, or Equal? EMC 3071 © Evan-Moor Corp.	Greater, Less, or Equal? EMC 3071 © Evan-Moor Corp.	Greater, Less, or Equal? EMC 3071 © Evan-Moor Corp.	Greater, Less, or Equal? EMC 3071 © Evan-Moor Corp.
Greater, Less, or Equal? EMC 3071 © Evan-Moor Corp.	Greater, Less, or Equal? EMC 3071 © Evan-Moor Corp.	Greater, Less, or Equal? EMC 3071 © Evan-Moor Corp.	Greater, Less, or Equal? EMC 3071 © Evan-Moor Corp.	Greater, Less, or Equal? EMC 3071 © Evan-Moor Corp.	Greater, Less, or Equal? EMC 3071 © Evan-Moor Corp.	Greater, Less, or Equal? EMC 3071 © Evan-Moor Corp.

Skip Counting

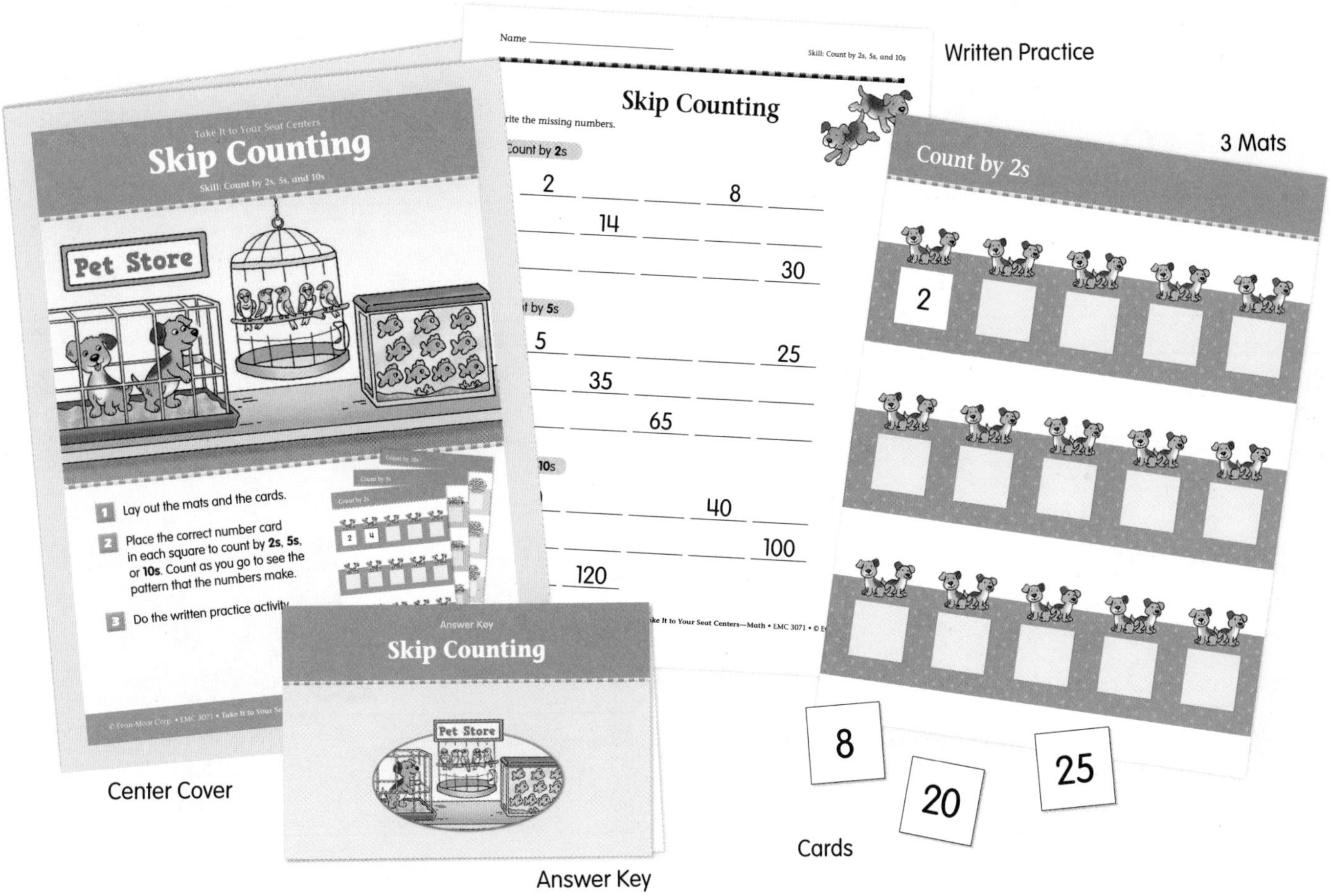

Skill: Count by 2s, 5s, and 10s

Steps to Follow

1. **Prepare the center.** (See page 3.)
2. **Introduce the center.** State the goal. Say: *You will place number cards on each mat in the correct order to count by 2s, 5s, and 10s.*
3. **Teach the skill.** Demonstrate how to use the center with individual students or small groups.
4. **Practice the skill.** Have students use the center independently or with a partner.

Contents

Written Practice............ 48
Center Cover.................. 49
Answer Key.................... 51
Center Mats 53, 55, 57
Cards 59

Name ______________________ Skill: Count by 2s, 5s, and 10s

Skip Counting

Write the missing numbers.

Count by **2**s

2	____	____	8	____
____	14	____	____	____
____	____	____	____	30

Count by **5**s

5	____	____	____	25
____	35	____	____	____
____	____	65	____	____

Count by **10**s

10	____	____	40	____
____	____	____	____	100
____	120			

Take It to Your Seat Centers

Skip Counting

Skill: Count by 2s, 5s, and 10s

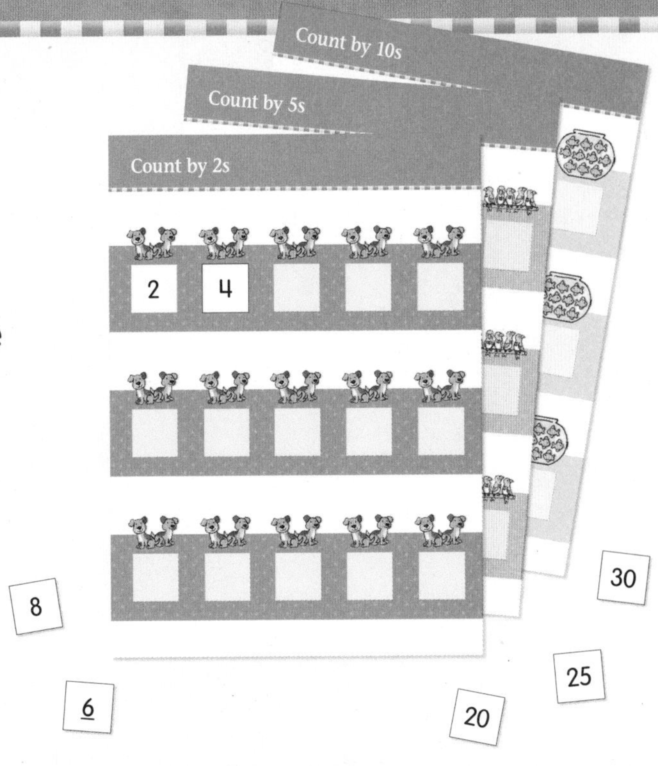

1 Lay out the mats and the cards.

2 Place the correct number card in each square to count by **2s**, **5s**, or **10s**. Count as you go to see the pattern that the numbers make.

3 Do the written practice activity.

(fold)

Answer Key

Skip Counting

Written Practice

Skip Counting

Write the missing numbers.

Count by 2s

2	4	6	**8**	10
12	**14**	16	18	20
22	24	26	28	**30**

Count by 5s

5	10	15	20	**25**
30	**35**	40	45	50
55	60	**65**	70	75

Count by 10s

10	20	30	**40**	50
60	70	80	90	**100**
110	**120**			

Answer Key

Skip Counting

Count by 2s

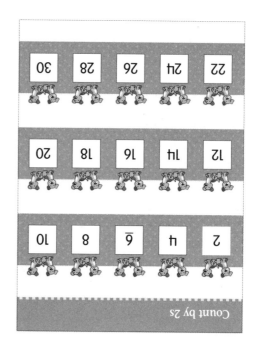

2	4	6	8	10
12	14	16	18	20
22	24	26	28	30

Count by 5s

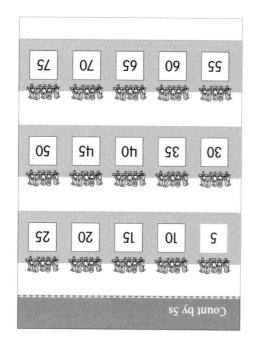

5	10	15	20	25
30	35	40	45	50
55	60	65	70	75

Count by 10s

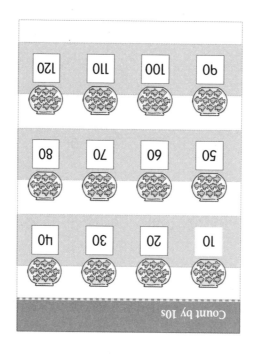

10	20	30	40
50	60	70	80
90	100	110	120

Count by 2s

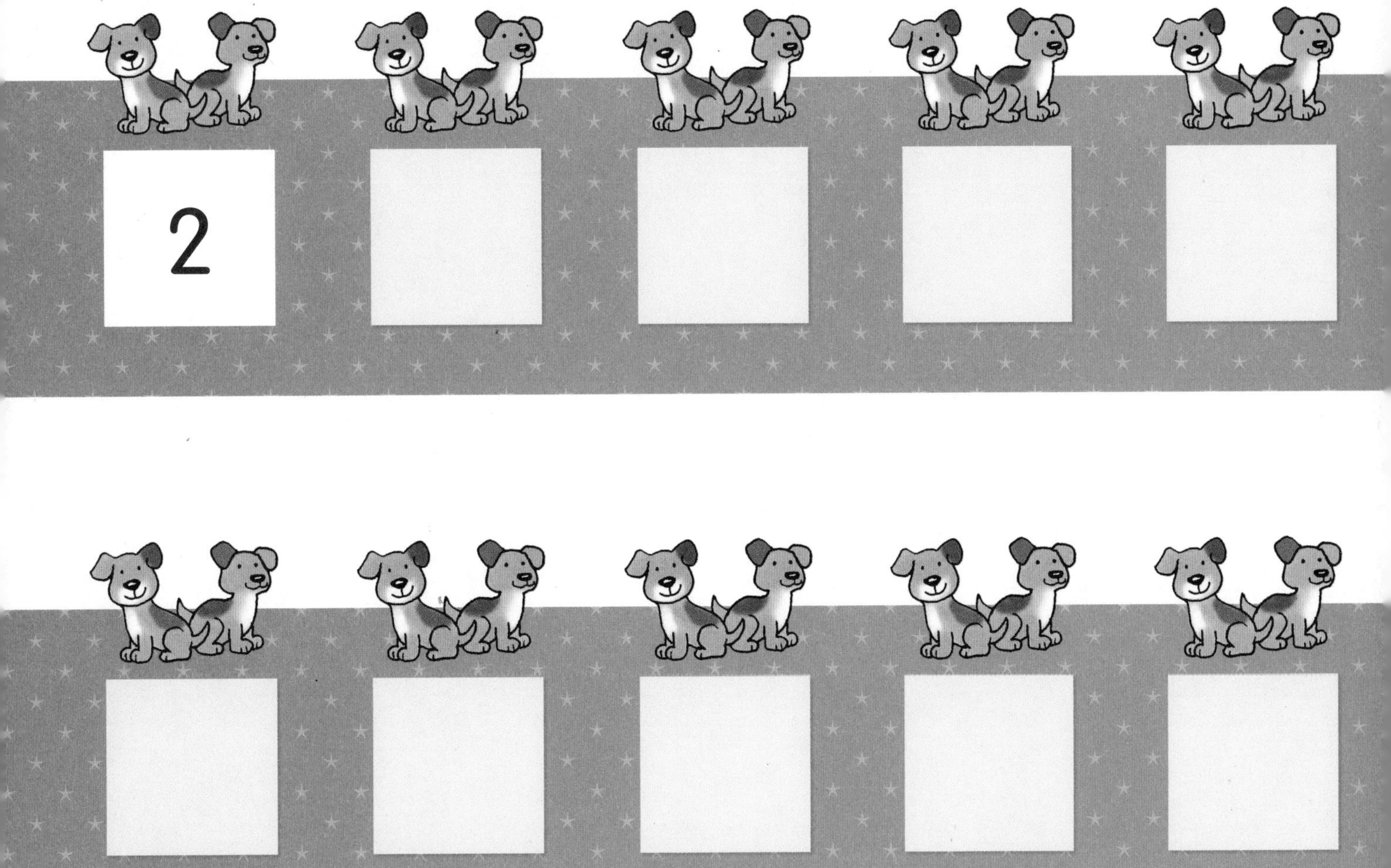

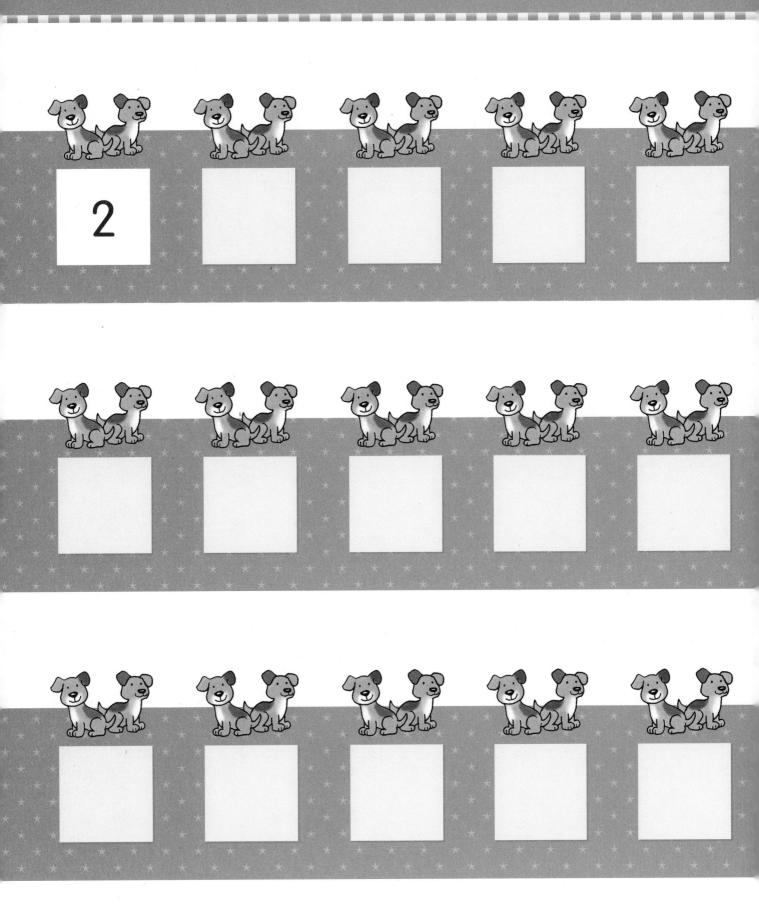

Count by 5s

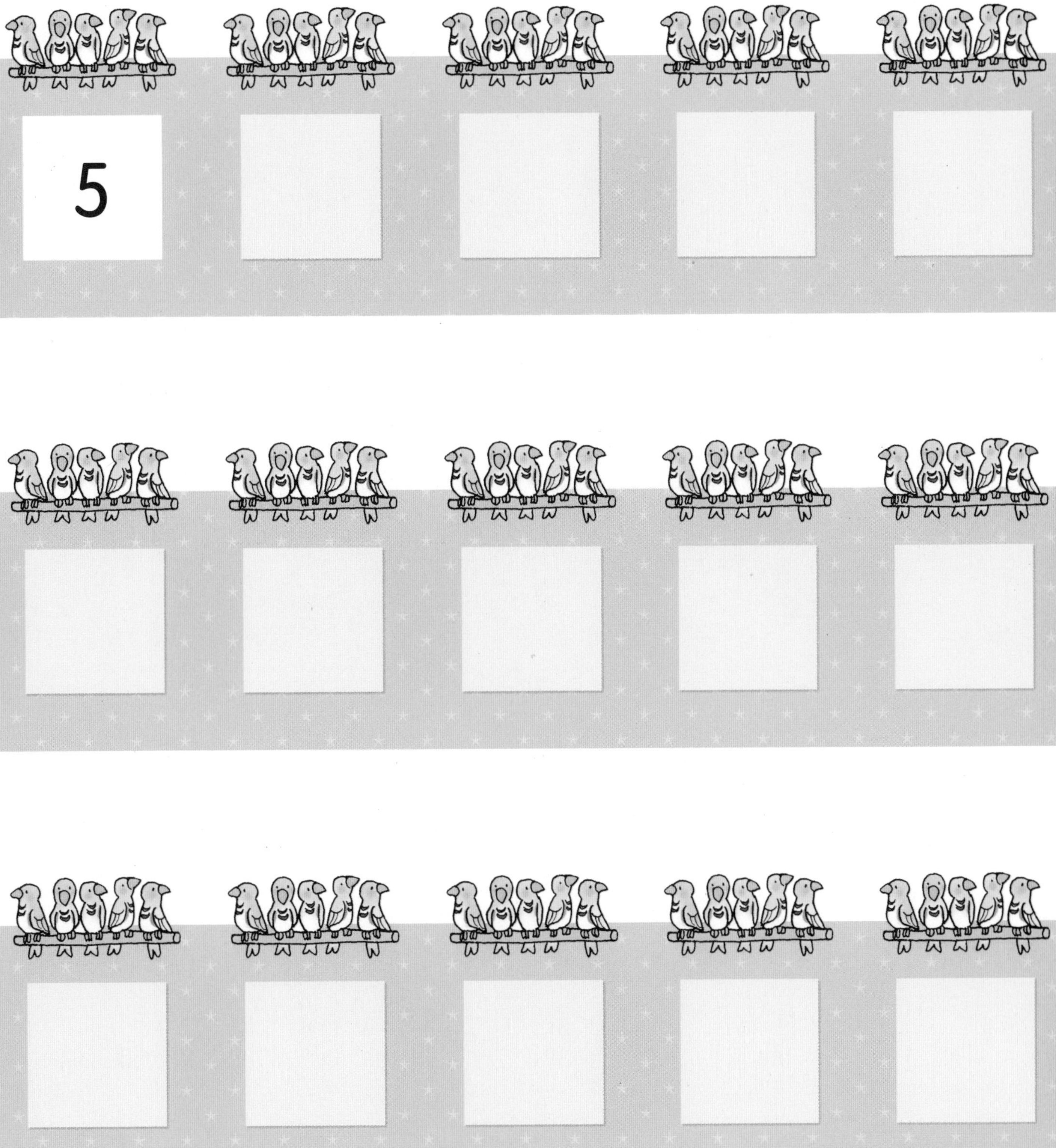

Count by 10s

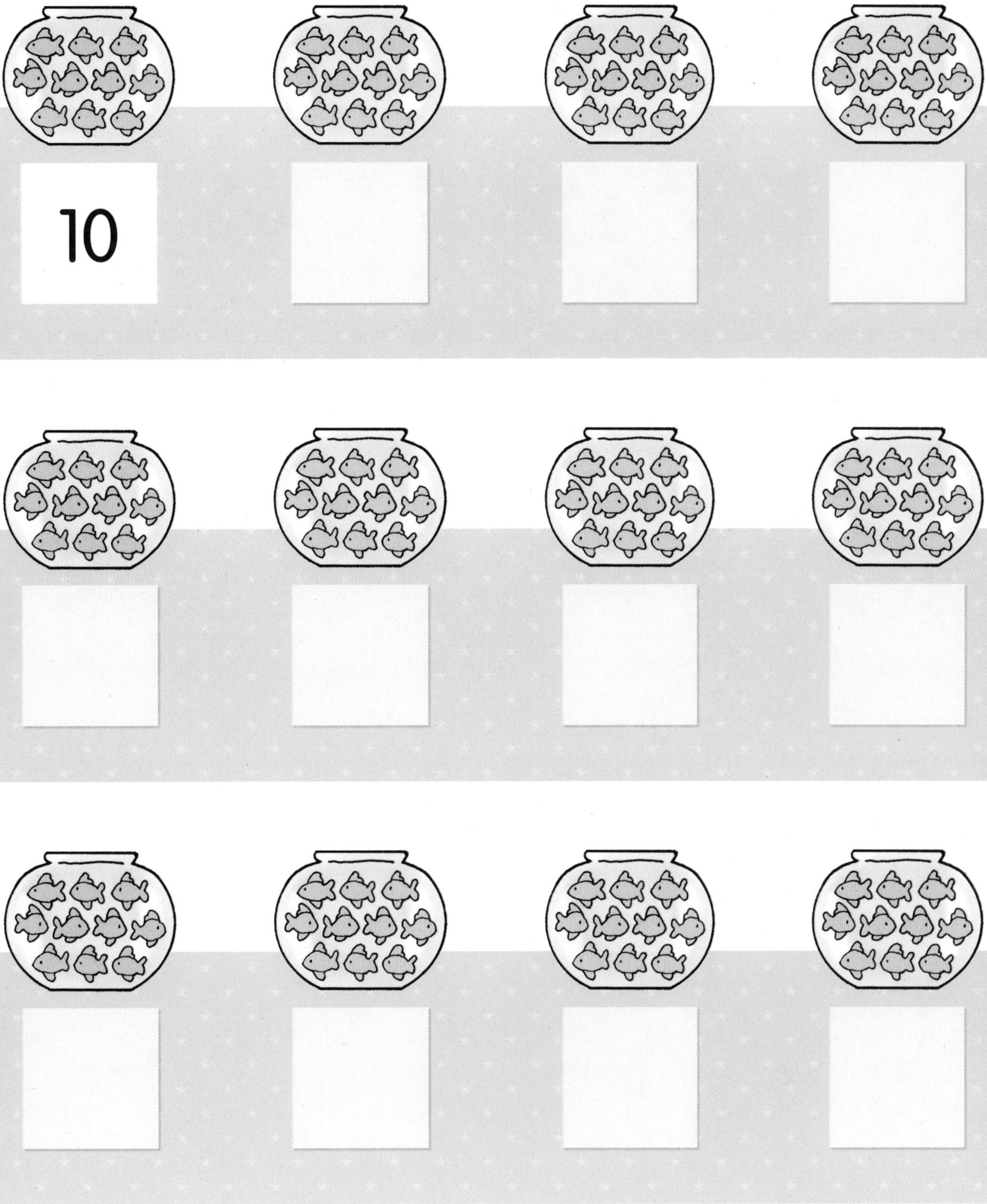

4	6	8	10	12	14
16	18	20	22	24	26
28	30	10	15	20	25
30	35	40	45	50	55
60	65	70	75	20	30
40	50	60	70	80	90
100	110	120			

Skip Counting	Skip Counting	Skip Counting	Skip Counting	Skip Counting	Skip Counting
EMC 3071	EMC 3071	EMC 3071	EMC 3071	EMC 3071	EMC 3071
© Evan-Moor Corp.	© Evan-Moor Corp.	© Evan-Moor Corp.	© Evan-Moor Corp.	© Evan-Moor Corp.	© Evan-Moor Corp.
Skip Counting	Skip Counting	Skip Counting	Skip Counting	Skip Counting	Skip Counting
EMC 3071	EMC 3071	EMC 3071	EMC 3071	EMC 3071	EMC 3071
© Evan-Moor Corp.	© Evan-Moor Corp.	© Evan-Moor Corp.	© Evan-Moor Corp.	© Evan-Moor Corp.	© Evan-Moor Corp.
Skip Counting	Skip Counting	Skip Counting	Skip Counting	Skip Counting	Skip Counting
EMC 3071	EMC 3071	EMC 3071	EMC 3071	EMC 3071	EMC 3071
© Evan-Moor Corp.	© Evan-Moor Corp.	© Evan-Moor Corp.	© Evan-Moor Corp.	© Evan-Moor Corp.	© Evan-Moor Corp.
Skip Counting	Skip Counting	Skip Counting	Skip Counting	Skip Counting	Skip Counting
EMC 3071	EMC 3071	EMC 3071	EMC 3071	EMC 3071	EMC 3071
© Evan-Moor Corp.	© Evan-Moor Corp.	© Evan-Moor Corp.	© Evan-Moor Corp.	© Evan-Moor Corp.	© Evan-Moor Corp.
Skip Counting	Skip Counting	Skip Counting	Skip Counting	Skip Counting	Skip Counting
EMC 3071	EMC 3071	EMC 3071	EMC 3071	EMC 3071	EMC 3071
© Evan-Moor Corp.	© Evan-Moor Corp.	© Evan-Moor Corp.	© Evan-Moor Corp.	© Evan-Moor Corp.	© Evan-Moor Corp.
Skip Counting	Skip Counting	Skip Counting	Skip Counting	Skip Counting	Skip Counting
EMC 3071	EMC 3071	EMC 3071	EMC 3071	EMC 3071	EMC 3071
© Evan-Moor Corp.	© Evan-Moor Corp.	© Evan-Moor Corp.	© Evan-Moor Corp.	© Evan-Moor Corp.	© Evan-Moor Corp.
			Skip Counting	Skip Counting	Skip Counting
			EMC 3071	EMC 3071	EMC 3071
			© Evan-Moor Corp.	© Evan-Moor Corp.	© Evan-Moor Corp.

Take It to Your Seat Centers

Add, Then Subtract

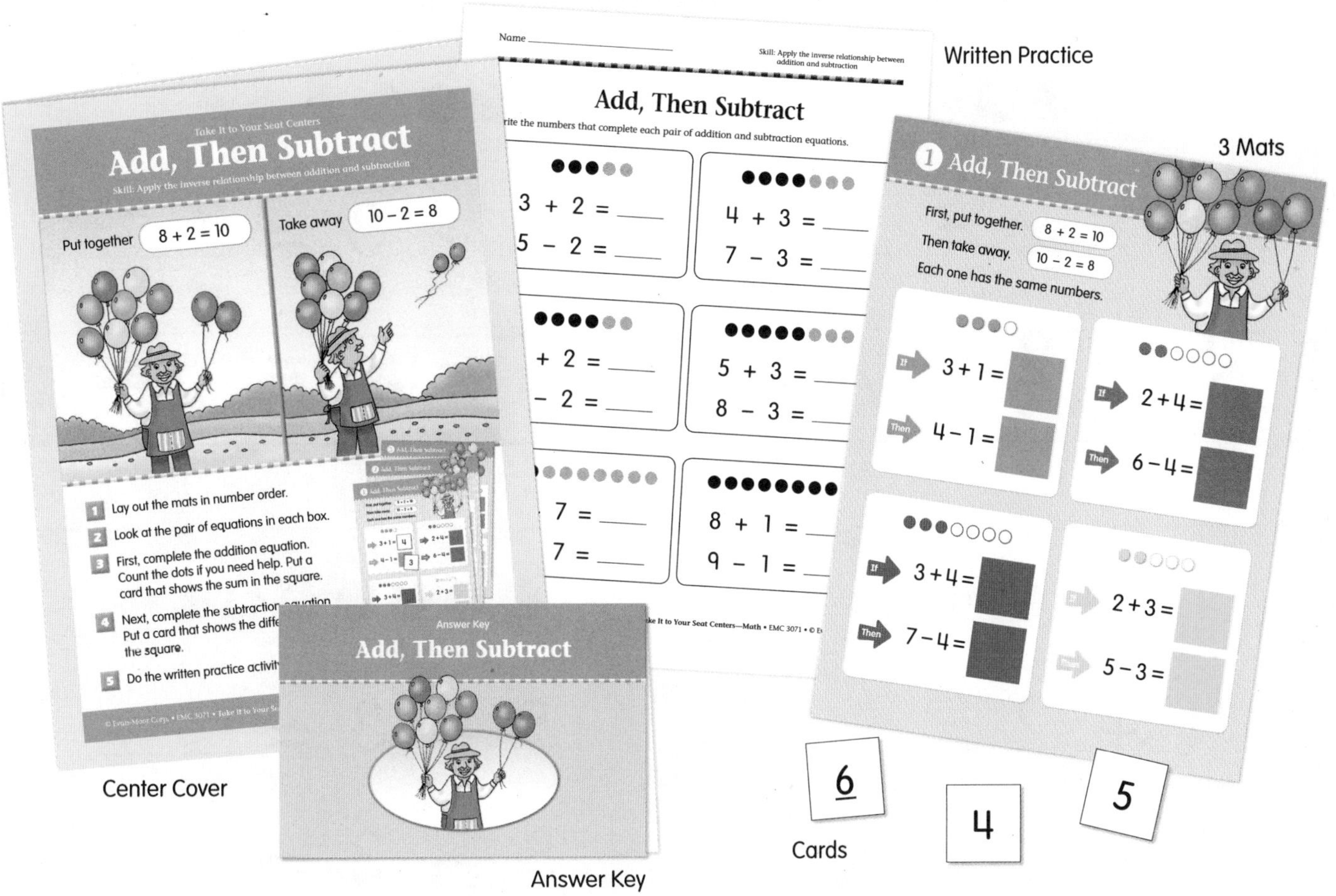

Skill: Apply the inverse relationship between addition and subtraction in facts to 10

Steps to Follow

1. **Prepare the center.** (See page 3.)
2. **Introduce the center.** State the goal. Say: *You will add and subtract the three numbers in a fact family to see how addition and subtraction are related.*
3. **Teach the skill.** Demonstrate how to use the center with individual students or small groups.
4. **Practice the skill.** Have students use the center independently or with a partner.

Contents

Written Practice 62
Center Cover 63
Answer Key 65
Center Mats 67, 69, 71
Cards 73

Name ______________________

Skill: Apply the inverse relationship between addition and subtraction

Add, Then Subtract

Write the numbers that complete each pair of addition and subtraction equations.

$3 + 2 =$ ____

$5 - 2 =$ ____

$4 + 3 =$ ____

$7 - 3 =$ ____

$4 + 2 =$ ____

$6 - 2 =$ ____

$5 + 3 =$ ____

$8 - 3 =$ ____

$3 + 7 =$ ____

$10 - 7 =$ ____

$8 + 1 =$ ____

$9 - 1 =$ ____

Add, Then Subtract

Skill: Apply the inverse relationship between addition and subtraction

1. Lay out the mats in number order.
2. Look at the pair of equations in each box.
3. First, complete the addition equation. Count the dots if you need help. Put a card that shows the sum in the square.
4. Next, complete the subtraction equation. Put a card that shows the difference in the square.
5. Do the written practice activity.

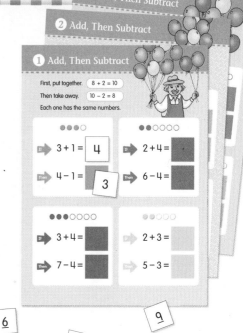

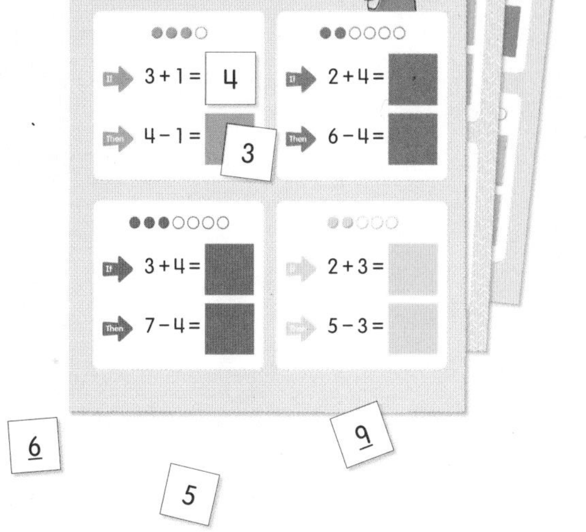

Written Practice

Add, Then Subtract

Write the numbers that complete each pair of addition and subtraction equations.

3 + 2 = 5
5 − 2 = 3

4 + 3 = 7
7 − 3 = 4

4 + 2 = 6
6 − 2 = 4

5 + 3 = 8
8 − 3 = 5

3 + 7 = 10
10 − 7 = 3

8 + 1 = 9
9 − 1 = 8

(fold)

Answer Key

Add, Then Subtract

Answer Key

Add, Then Subtract

1 Add, Then Subtract

First, put together. 8 + 2 = 10

Then take away. 10 − 2 = 8

Each one has the same numbers.

- If 3 + 1 = 4, Then 4 − 1 = 3
- If 2 + 4 = 6, Then 6 − 4 = 2
- If 3 + 4 = 7, Then 7 − 4 = 3
- If 2 + 3 = 5, Then 5 − 3 = 2

2 Add, Then Subtract

- If 5 + 2 = 7, Then 7 − 2 = 5
- If 5 + 4 = 9, Then 9 − 4 = 5
- If 4 + 4 = 8, Then 8 − 4 = 4
- If 6 + 3 = 9, Then 9 − 3 = 6

3 Add, Then Subtract

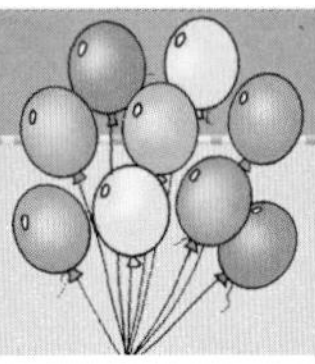

- If 2 + 6 = 8, Then 8 − 6 = 2
- If 2 + 7 = 9, Then 9 − 7 = 2
- If 6 + 4 = 10, Then 10 − 4 = 6
- If 8 + 2 = 10, Then 10 − 2 = 8

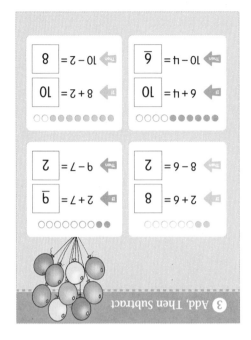

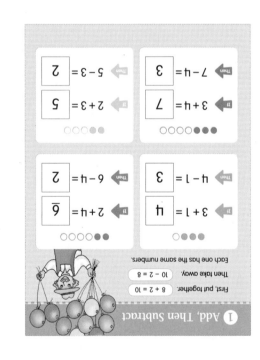

1 Add, Then Subtract

First, put together. 8 + 2 = 10

Then take away. 10 − 2 = 8

Each one has the same numbers.

If 3 + 1 =

Then 4 − 1 =

If 2 + 4 =

Then 6 − 4 =

If 3 + 4 =

Then 7 − 4 =

If 2 + 3 =

Then 5 − 3 =

2 Add, Then Subtract

If $5 + 2 = \square$

Then $7 - 2 = \square$

If $5 + 4 = \square$

Then $9 - 4 = \square$

If $4 + 4 = \square$

Then $8 - 4 = \square$

If $6 + 3 = \square$

Then $9 - 3 = \square$

3 Add, Then Subtract

If $2 + 6 =$ ☐

Then $8 - 6 =$ ☐

If $2 + 7 =$ ☐

Then $9 - 7 =$ ☐

If $6 + 4 =$ ☐

Then $10 - 4 =$ ☐

If $8 + 2 =$ ☐

Then $10 - 2 =$ ☐

2	2	2	2	2
3	3	3	3	3
4	4	4	4	4
5	5	5	5	5
6	6	6	6	6
7	7	7	7	7
8	8	8	8	8
9	9	9	9	9
10	10	10	10	10

Add, Then Subtract EMC 3071 © Evan-Moor Corp.	Add, Then Subtract EMC 3071 © Evan-Moor Corp.	Add, Then Subtract EMC 3071 © Evan-Moor Corp.	Add, Then Subtract EMC 3071 © Evan-Moor Corp.	Add, Then Subtract EMC 3071 © Evan-Moor Corp.
Add, Then Subtract EMC 3071 © Evan-Moor Corp.	Add, Then Subtract EMC 3071 © Evan-Moor Corp.	Add, Then Subtract EMC 3071 © Evan-Moor Corp.	Add, Then Subtract EMC 3071 © Evan-Moor Corp.	Add, Then Subtract EMC 3071 © Evan-Moor Corp.
Add, Then Subtract EMC 3071 © Evan-Moor Corp.	Add, Then Subtract EMC 3071 © Evan-Moor Corp.	Add, Then Subtract EMC 3071 © Evan-Moor Corp.	Add, Then Subtract EMC 3071 © Evan-Moor Corp.	Add, Then Subtract EMC 3071 © Evan-Moor Corp.
Add, Then Subtract EMC 3071 © Evan-Moor Corp.	Add, Then Subtract EMC 3071 © Evan-Moor Corp.	Add, Then Subtract EMC 3071 © Evan-Moor Corp.	Add, Then Subtract EMC 3071 © Evan-Moor Corp.	Add, Then Subtract EMC 3071 © Evan-Moor Corp.
Add, Then Subtract EMC 3071 © Evan-Moor Corp.	Add, Then Subtract EMC 3071 © Evan-Moor Corp.	Add, Then Subtract EMC 3071 © Evan-Moor Corp.	Add, Then Subtract EMC 3071 © Evan-Moor Corp.	Add, Then Subtract EMC 3071 © Evan-Moor Corp.
Add, Then Subtract EMC 3071 © Evan-Moor Corp.	Add, Then Subtract EMC 3071 © Evan-Moor Corp.	Add, Then Subtract EMC 3071 © Evan-Moor Corp.	Add, Then Subtract EMC 3071 © Evan-Moor Corp.	Add, Then Subtract EMC 3071 © Evan-Moor Corp.
Add, Then Subtract EMC 3071 © Evan-Moor Corp.	Add, Then Subtract EMC 3071 © Evan-Moor Corp.	Add, Then Subtract EMC 3071 © Evan-Moor Corp.	Add, Then Subtract EMC 3071 © Evan-Moor Corp.	Add, Then Subtract EMC 3071 © Evan-Moor Corp.
Add, Then Subtract EMC 3071 © Evan-Moor Corp.	Add, Then Subtract EMC 3071 © Evan-Moor Corp.	Add, Then Subtract EMC 3071 © Evan-Moor Corp.	Add, Then Subtract EMC 3071 © Evan-Moor Corp.	Add, Then Subtract EMC 3071 © Evan-Moor Corp.
Add, Then Subtract EMC 3071 © Evan-Moor Corp.	Add, Then Subtract EMC 3071 © Evan-Moor Corp.	Add, Then Subtract EMC 3071 © Evan-Moor Corp.	Add, Then Subtract EMC 3071 © Evan-Moor Corp.	Add, Then Subtract EMC 3071 © Evan-Moor Corp.

Take It to Your Seat Centers

Jump Up to Add

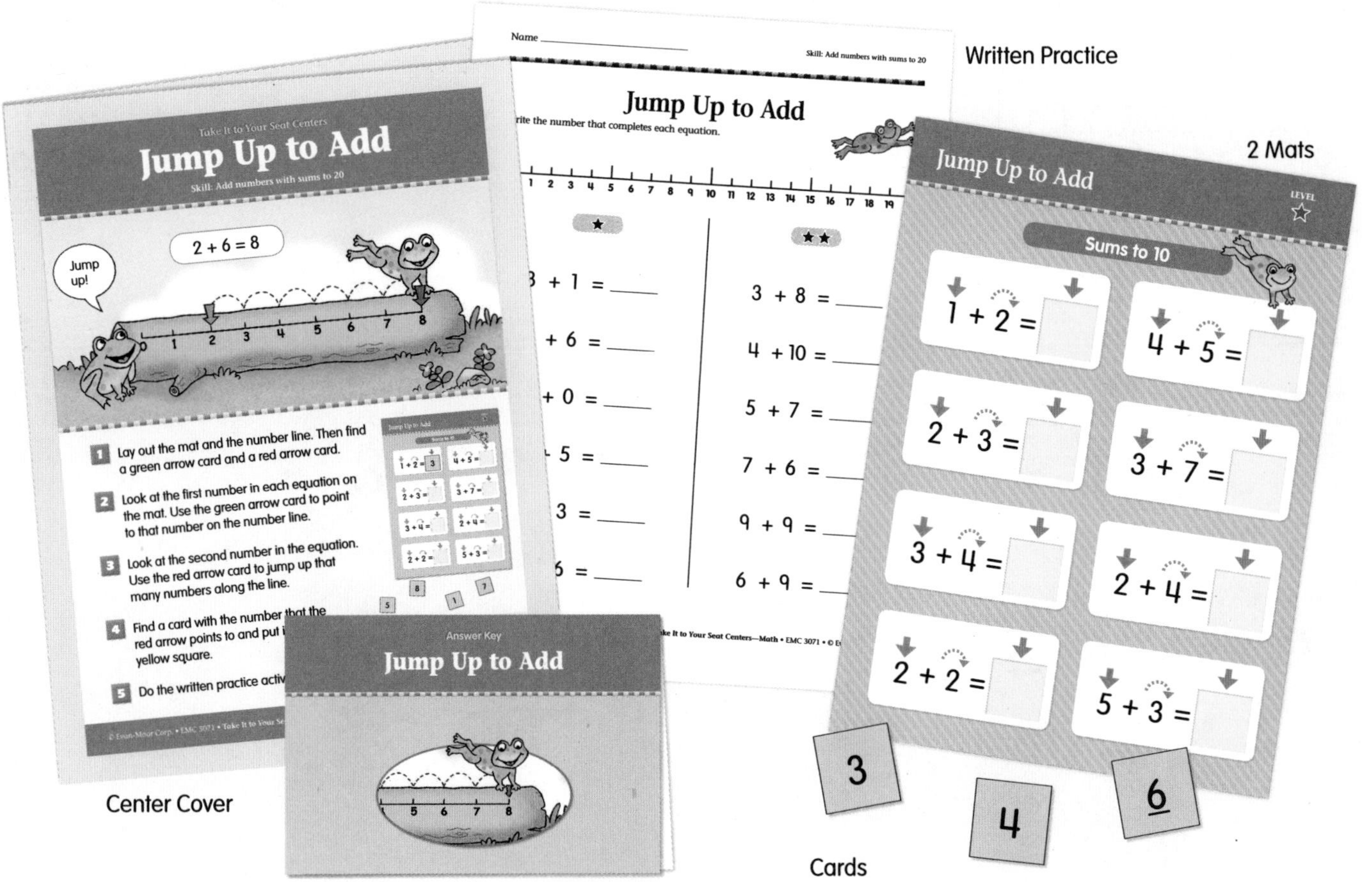

Written Practice

2 Mats

Center Cover

Cards

Answer Key

Skill: Add numbers with sums to 20

Steps to Follow

1. **Prepare the center.** (See page 3.)
2. **Introduce the center.** State the goal. Say: *You will move an arrow along a number line to help you find the sum for each addition equation.*
3. **Teach the skill.** Demonstrate how to use the center with individual students or small groups.
4. **Practice the skill.** Have students use the center independently or with a partner.

Contents

Written Practice............ 76

Center Cover.................. 77

Answer Key..................... 79

Center Mats

Level 1......................... 81

Level 2......................... 83

Cards.............................. 85

Name ____________________ Skill: Add numbers with sums to 20

Jump Up to Add

Write the number that completes each equation.

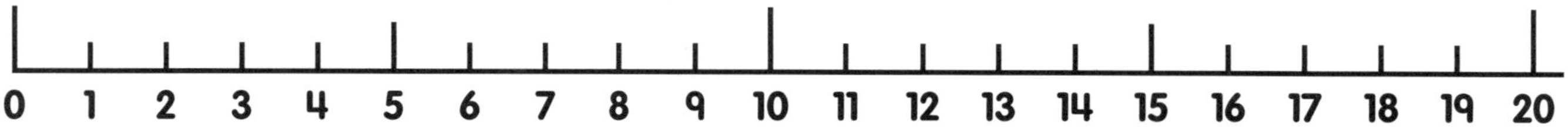

★

3 + 1 = ______

2 + 6 = ______

5 + 0 = ______

2 + 5 = ______

6 + 3 = ______

4 + 6 = ______

★★

3 + 8 = ______

4 + 10 = ______

5 + 7 = ______

7 + 6 = ______

9 + 9 = ______

6 + 9 = ______

Jump Up to Add

Skill: Add numbers with sums to 20

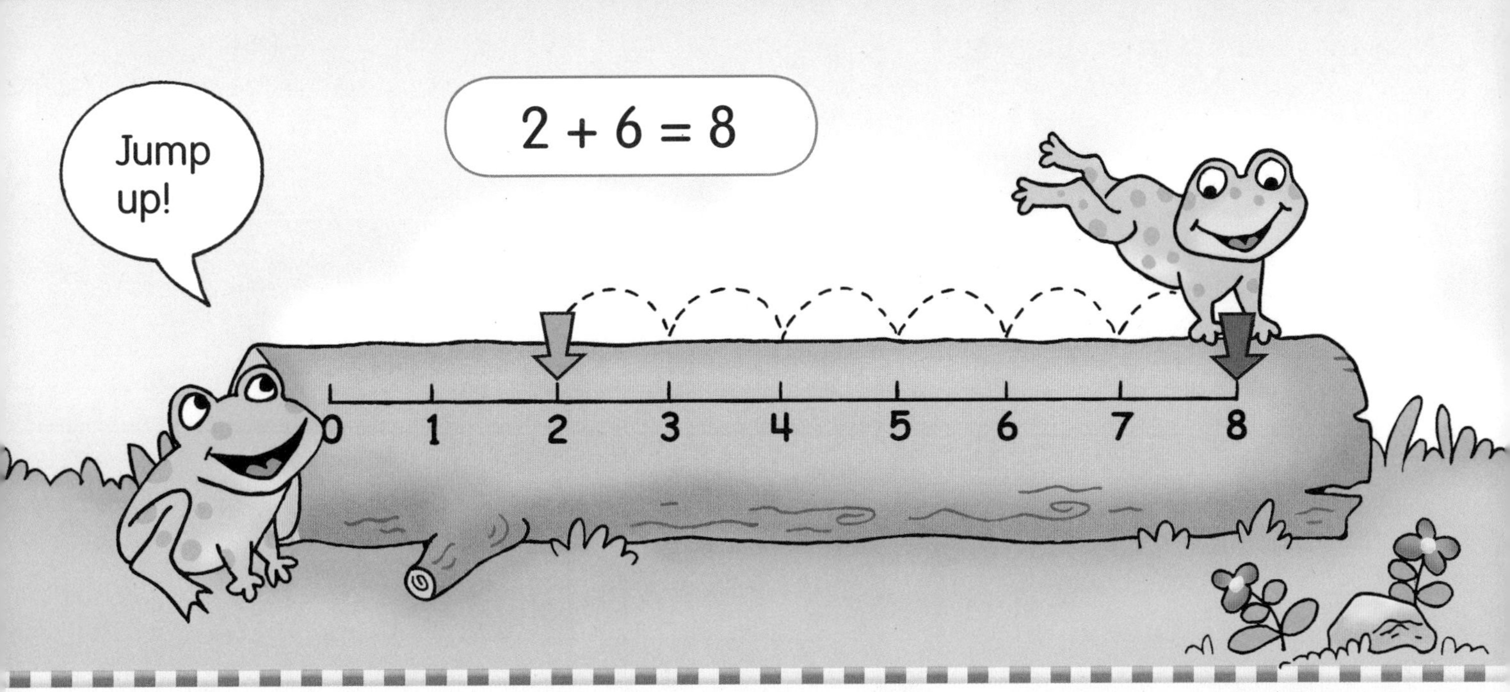

1. Lay out the mat and the number line. Then find a green arrow card and a red arrow card.
2. Look at the first number in each equation on the mat. Use the green arrow card to point to that number on the number line.
3. Look at the second number in the equation. Use the red arrow card to jump up that many numbers along the line.
4. Find a card with the number that the red arrow points to and put it in the yellow square.
5. Do the written practice activity.

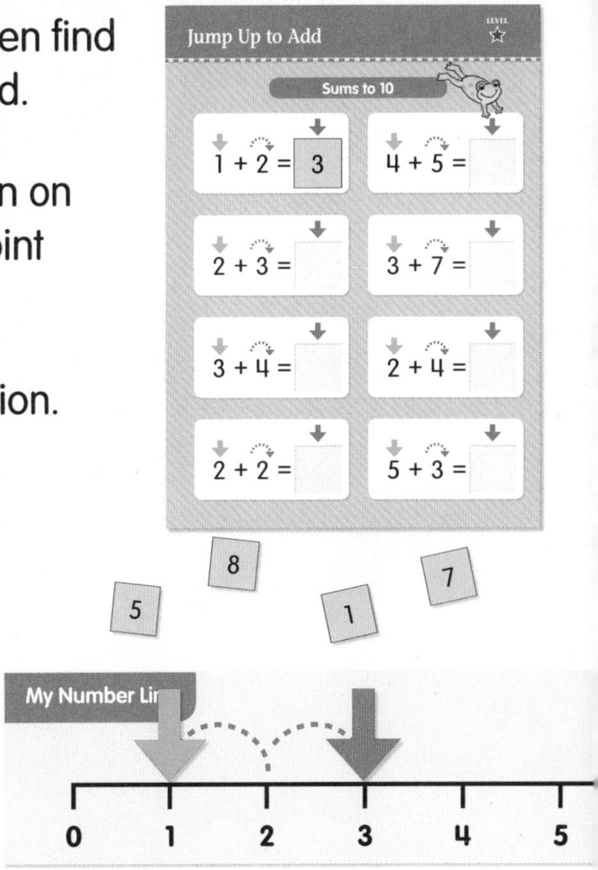

Answer Key

Jump Up to Add

(fold)

Written Practice

Jump Up to Add

Write the number that completes each equation.

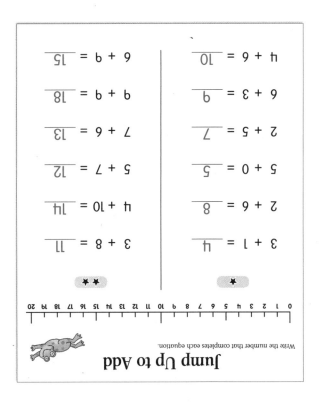

0 1 2 3 4 5 6 7 8 9 10 11 12 13 14 15 16 17 18 19 20

★

3 + 1 = 4

2 + 6 = 8

5 + 0 = 5

2 + 5 = 7

6 + 3 = 9

4 + 6 = 10

★★

3 + 8 = 11

4 + 10 = 14

5 + 7 = 12

7 + 6 = 13

9 + 9 = 18

6 + 9 = 15

Answer Key

Jump Up to Add

Jump Up to Add

LEVEL ☆

Sums to 10

1 + 2 = 3	4 + 5 = 9
2 + 3 = 5	3 + 7 = 10
3 + 4 = 7	2 + 4 = 6
2 + 2 = 4	5 + 3 = 8

Jump Up to Add

LEVEL ☆☆

Sums from 11 to 20

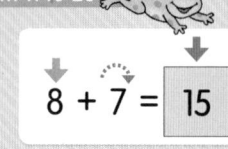

6 + 5 = 11	8 + 7 = 15
5 + 8 = 13	10 + 10 = 20
9 + 9 = 18	9 + 8 = 17
7 + 9 = 16	10 + 2 = 12

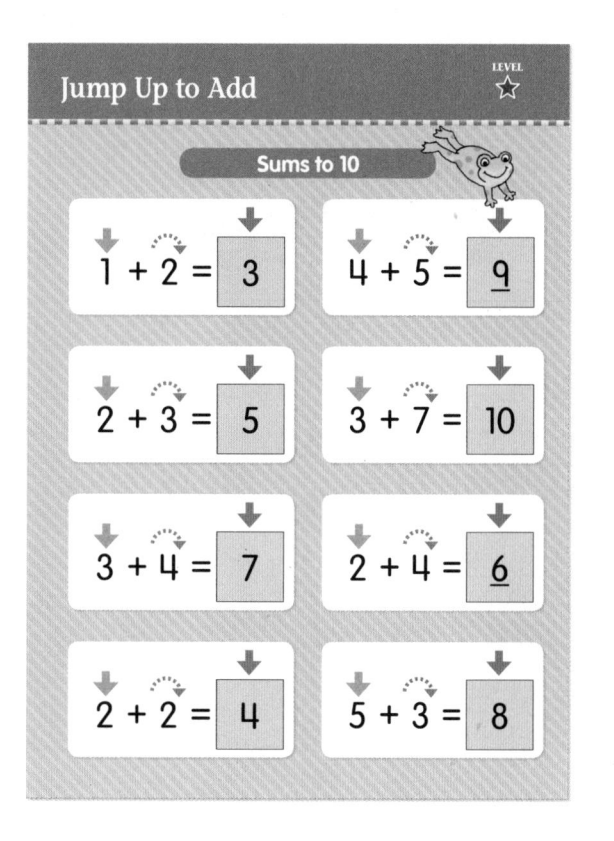

Jump Up to Add

LEVEL ☆

Sums to 10

1 + 2 =

4 + 5 =

2 + 3 =

3 + 7 =

3 + 4 =

2 + 4 =

2 + 2 =

5 + 3 =

Jump Up to Add

LEVEL ★★

Sums from 11 to 20

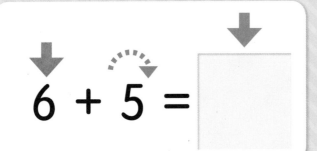

6 + 5 = ☐

8 + 7 = ☐

5 + 8 = ☐

10 + 10 = ☐

9 + 9 = ☐

9 + 8 = ☐

7 + 9 = ☐

10 + 2 = ☐

1	2	3	3
4	4	5	5
6	6	7	7
8	8	9	10
11	12	13	13
14	14	15	15
16	16	17	17
18	18	19	20

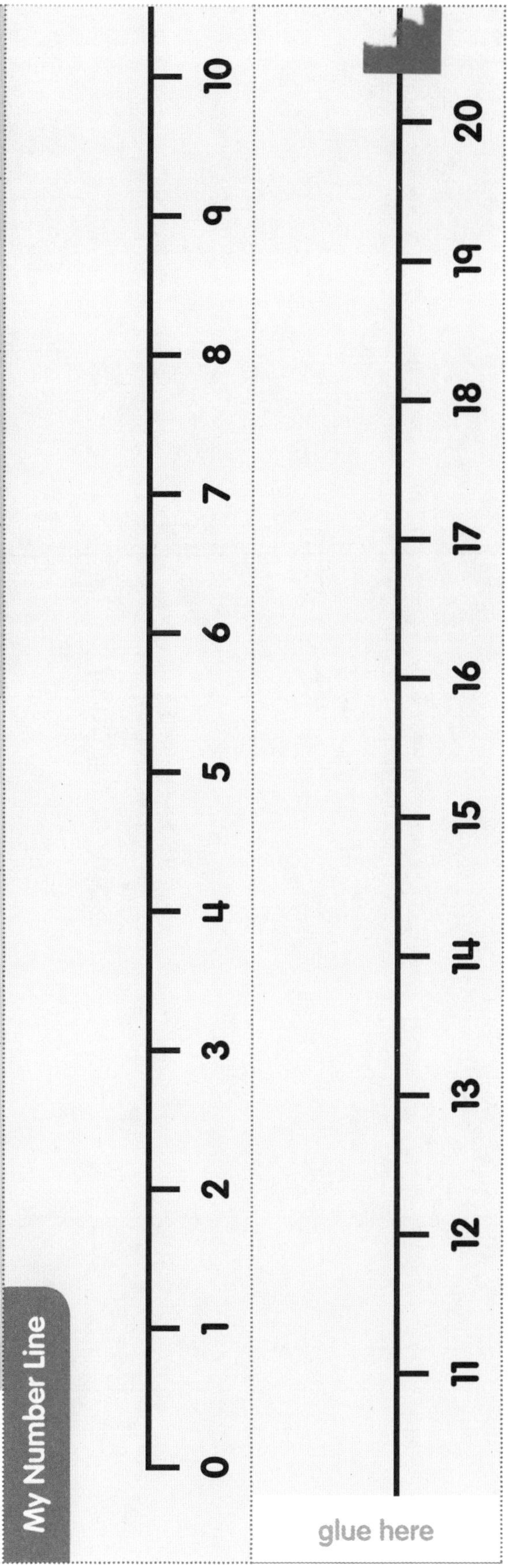

Jump Up to Add EMC 3071 © Evan-Moor Corp.	Jump Up to Add EMC 3071 © Evan-Moor Corp.	Jump Up to Add EMC 3071 © Evan-Moor Corp.	Jump Up to Add EMC 3071 © Evan-Moor Corp.
Jump Up to Add EMC 3071 © Evan-Moor Corp.	Jump Up to Add EMC 3071 © Evan-Moor Corp.	Jump Up to Add EMC 3071 © Evan-Moor Corp.	Jump Up to Add EMC 3071 © Evan-Moor Corp.
Jump Up to Add EMC 3071 © Evan-Moor Corp.	Jump Up to Add EMC 3071 © Evan-Moor Corp.	Jump Up to Add EMC 3071 © Evan-Moor Corp.	Jump Up to Add EMC 3071 © Evan-Moor Corp.
Jump Up to Add EMC 3071 © Evan-Moor Corp.	Jump Up to Add EMC 3071 © Evan-Moor Corp.	Jump Up to Add EMC 3071 © Evan-Moor Corp.	Jump Up to Add EMC 3071 © Evan-Moor Corp.
Jump Up to Add EMC 3071 © Evan-Moor Corp.	Jump Up to Add EMC 3071 © Evan-Moor Corp.	Jump Up to Add EMC 3071 © Evan-Moor Corp.	Jump Up to Add EMC 3071 © Evan-Moor Corp.
Jump Up to Add EMC 3071 © Evan-Moor Corp.	Jump Up to Add EMC 3071 © Evan-Moor Corp.	Jump Up to Add EMC 3071 © Evan-Moor Corp.	Jump Up to Add EMC 3071 © Evan-Moor Corp.
Jump Up to Add EMC 3071 © Evan-Moor Corp.	Jump Up to Add EMC 3071 © Evan-Moor Corp.	Jump Up to Add EMC 3071 © Evan-Moor Corp.	Jump Up to Add EMC 3071 © Evan-Moor Corp.
Jump Up to Add EMC 3071 © Evan-Moor Corp.	Jump Up to Add EMC 3071 © Evan-Moor Corp.	Jump Up to Add EMC 3071 © Evan-Moor Corp.	Jump Up to Add EMC 3071 © Evan-Moor Corp.
Jump Up to Add EMC 3071 © Evan-Moor Corp.	Jump Up to Add EMC 3071 © Evan-Moor Corp.	Jump Up to Add EMC 3071 © Evan-Moor Corp.	Jump Up to Add EMC 3071 © Evan-Moor Corp.

Jump Up to Add
EMC 3071
© Evan-Moor Corp.

Jump Up to Add
EMC 3071
© Evan-Moor Corp.

Jump Back to Subtract

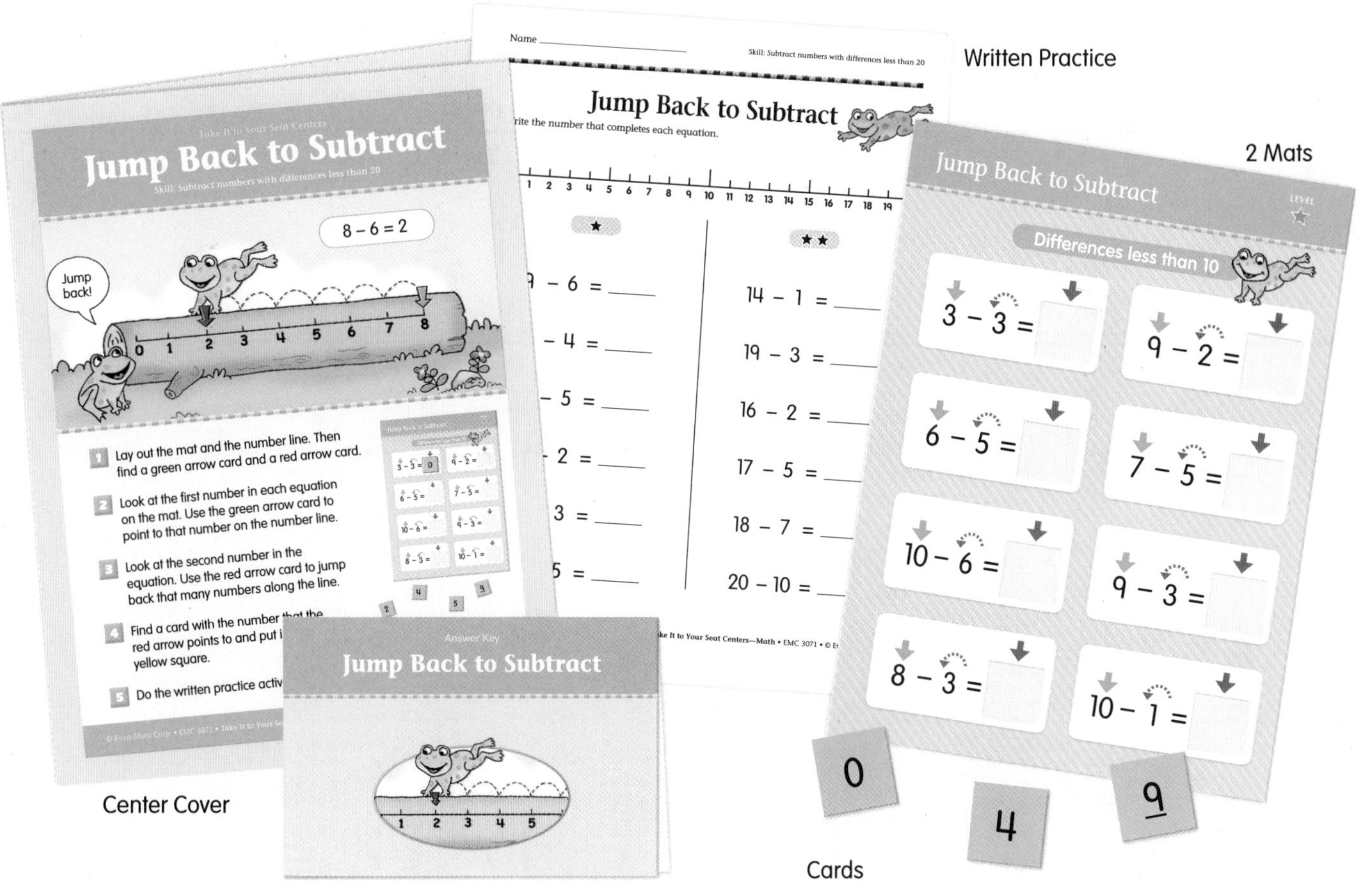

Skill: Subtract numbers with differences less than 20

Steps to Follow

1. **Prepare the center.** (See page 3.)
2. **Introduce the center.** State the goal. Say: *You will move an arrow along a number line to help you find the difference for each subtraction equation.*
3. **Teach the skill.** Demonstrate how to use the center with individual students or small groups.
4. **Practice the skill.** Have students use the center independently or with a partner.

Contents

Written Practice............ 88
Center Cover.................. 89
Answer Key.................... 91
Center Mats
Level 1........................ 93
Level 2........................ 95
Cards............................ 97

Name ______________________

Skill: Subtract numbers with differences less than 20

Jump Back to Subtract

Write the number that completes each equation.

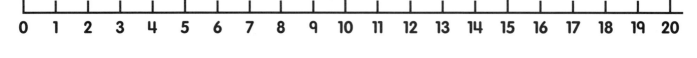

★	★★
9 – 6 = ____	14 – 1 = ____
6 – 4 = ____	19 – 3 = ____
10 – 5 = ____	16 – 2 = ____
8 – 2 = ____	17 – 5 = ____
7 – 3 = ____	18 – 7 = ____
5 – 5 = ____	20 – 10 = ____

Take It to Your Seat Centers

Jump Back to Subtract

Skill: Subtract numbers with differences less than 20

1. Lay out the mat and the number line. Then find a green arrow card and a red arrow card.
2. Look at the first number in each equation on the mat. Use the green arrow card to point to that number on the number line.
3. Look at the second number in the equation. Use the red arrow card to jump back that many numbers along the line.
4. Find a card with the number that the red arrow points to and put it in the yellow square.
5. Do the written practice activity.

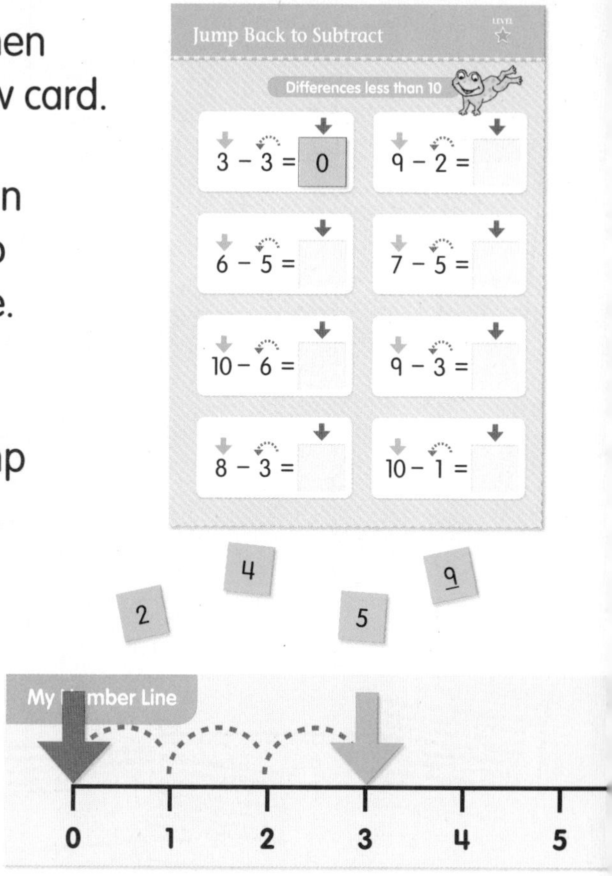

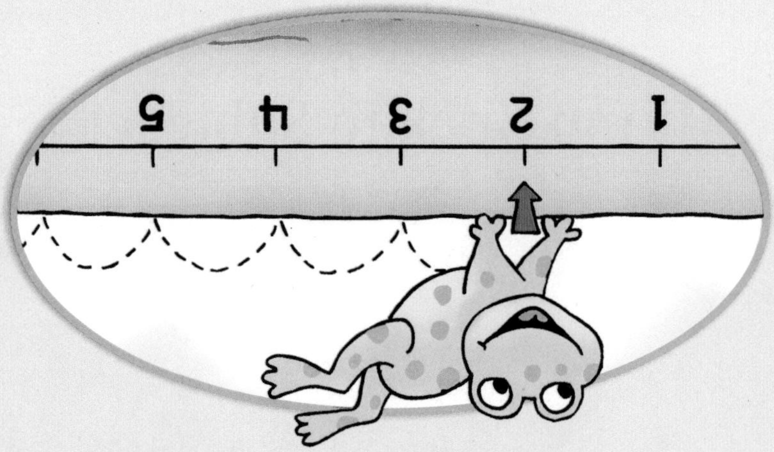

Jump Back to Subtract

Answer Key

(fold)

Written Practice

Jump Back to Subtract

Write the number that completes each equation.

0 1 2 3 4 5 6 7 8 9 10 11 12 13 14 15 16 17 18 19 20

★	★★
9 − 6 = 3	14 − 1 = 13
6 − 4 = 2	19 − 3 = 16
10 − 5 = 5	16 − 2 = 14
8 − 2 = 6	17 − 5 = 12
7 − 3 = 4	18 − 7 = 11
5 − 5 = 0	20 − 10 = 10

Answer Key

Jump Back to Subtract

Jump Back to Subtract

LEVEL ☆

Differences less than 10

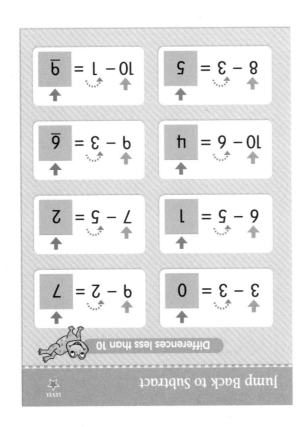

3 − 3 = 0	9 − 2 = 7
6 − 5 = 1	7 − 5 = 2
10 − 6 = 4	9 − 3 = 6
8 − 3 = 5	10 − 1 = 9

Jump Back to Subtract

LEVEL ☆☆

Differences less than 20

19 − 8 = 11	17 − 5 = 12
18 − 4 = 14	14 − 4 = 10
16 − 3 = 13	19 − 1 = 18
18 − 2 = 16	20 − 3 = 17

Jump Back to Subtract

LEVEL ☆

Differences less than 10

$3 - 3 = \square$

$9 - 2 = \square$

$6 - 5 = \square$

$7 - 5 = \square$

$10 - 6 = \square$

$9 - 3 = \square$

$8 - 3 = \square$

$10 - 1 = \square$

Jump Back to Subtract

LEVEL ☆☆

Differences less than 20

$19 - 8 = \square$

$17 - 5 = \square$

$18 - 4 = \square$

$14 - 4 = \square$

$16 - 3 = \square$

$19 - 1 = \square$

$18 - 2 = \square$

$20 - 3 = \square$

0	1	2	3
4	4	5	5
6	6	7	7
8	8	9	10
10	11	12	13
14	14	15	15
16	16	17	17
18	18	19	20

My Number Line

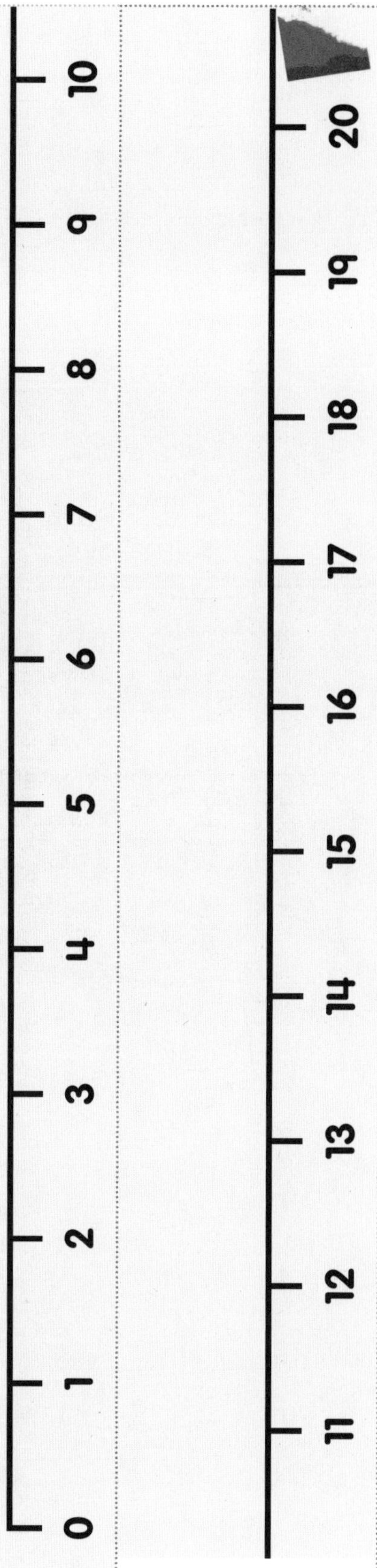

glue here

Jump Back to Subtract
EMC 3071
© Evan-Moor Corp.

Jump Back to Subtract
EMC 3071
© Evan-Moor Corp.

Jump Back to Subtract EMC 3071 © Evan-Moor Corp.	Jump Back to Subtract EMC 3071 © Evan-Moor Corp.	Jump Back to Subtract EMC 3071 © Evan-Moor Corp.	Jump Back to Subtract EMC 3071 © Evan-Moor Corp.
Jump Back to Subtract EMC 3071 © Evan-Moor Corp.	Jump Back to Subtract EMC 3071 © Evan-Moor Corp.	Jump Back to Subtract EMC 3071 © Evan-Moor Corp.	Jump Back to Subtract EMC 3071 © Evan-Moor Corp.
Jump Back to Subtract EMC 3071 © Evan-Moor Corp.	Jump Back to Subtract EMC 3071 © Evan-Moor Corp.	Jump Back to Subtract EMC 3071 © Evan-Moor Corp.	Jump Back to Subtract EMC 3071 © Evan-Moor Corp.
Jump Back to Subtract EMC 3071 © Evan-Moor Corp.	Jump Back to Subtract EMC 3071 © Evan-Moor Corp.	Jump Back to Subtract EMC 3071 © Evan-Moor Corp.	Jump Back to Subtract EMC 3071 © Evan-Moor Corp.
Jump Back to Subtract EMC 3071 © Evan-Moor Corp.	Jump Back to Subtract EMC 3071 © Evan-Moor Corp.	Jump Back to Subtract EMC 3071 © Evan-Moor Corp.	Jump Back to Subtract EMC 3071 © Evan-Moor Corp.
Jump Back to Subtract EMC 3071 © Evan-Moor Corp.	Jump Back to Subtract EMC 3071 © Evan-Moor Corp.	Jump Back to Subtract EMC 3071 © Evan-Moor Corp.	Jump Back to Subtract EMC 3071 © Evan-Moor Corp.
Jump Back to Subtract EMC 3071 © Evan-Moor Corp.	Jump Back to Subtract EMC 3071 © Evan-Moor Corp.	Jump Back to Subtract EMC 3071 © Evan-Moor Corp.	Jump Back to Subtract EMC 3071 © Evan-Moor Corp.
Jump Back to Subtract EMC 3071 © Evan-Moor Corp.	Jump Back to Subtract EMC 3071 © Evan-Moor Corp.	Jump Back to Subtract EMC 3071 © Evan-Moor Corp.	Jump Back to Subtract EMC 3071 © Evan-Moor Corp.
Jump Back to Subtract EMC 3071 © Evan-Moor Corp.	Jump Back to Subtract EMC 3071 © Evan-Moor Corp.	Jump Back to Subtract EMC 3071 © Evan-Moor Corp.	Jump Back to Subtract EMC 3071 © Evan-Moor Corp.

Measure It

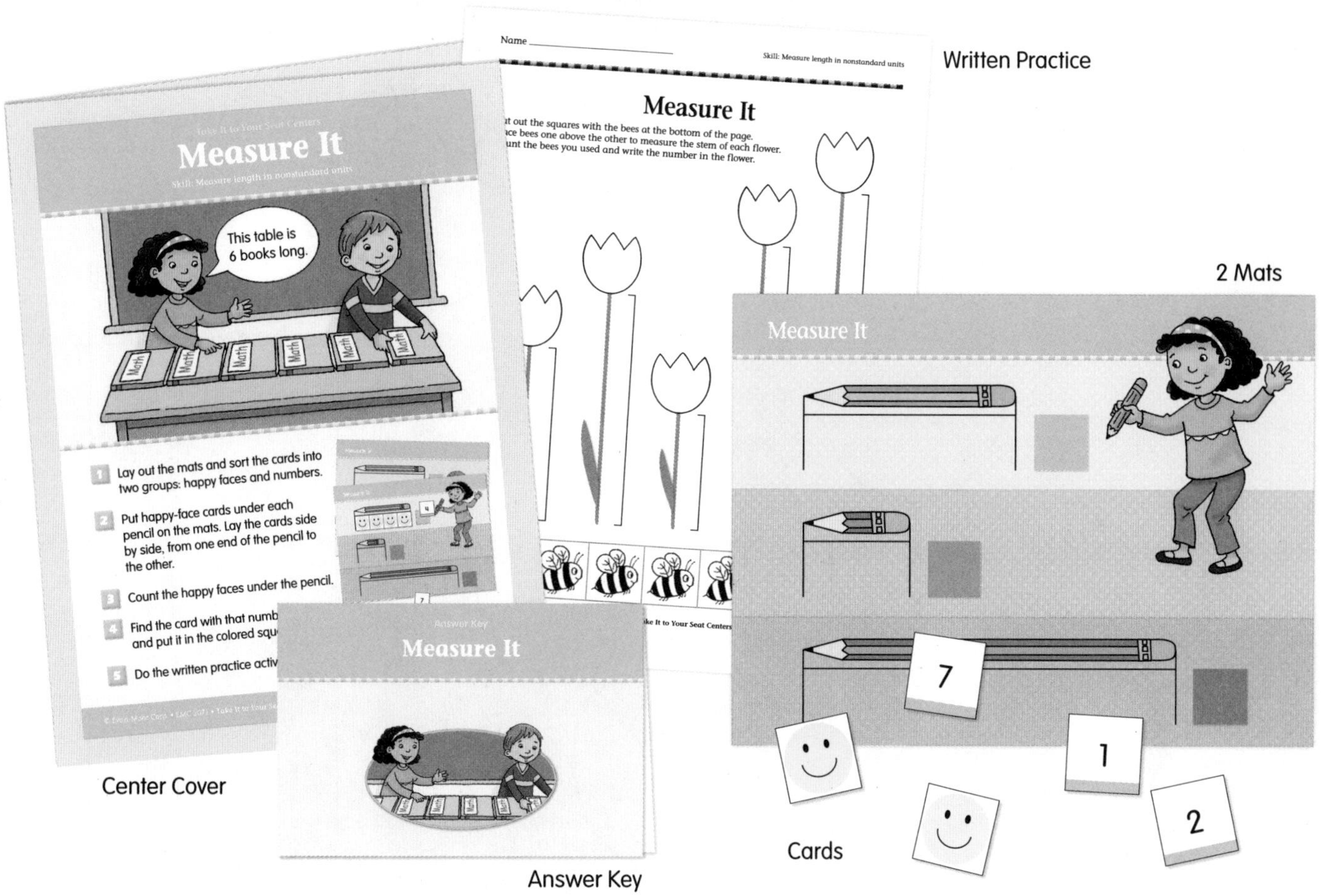

Skill: Measure length in nonstandard units

Steps to Follow

1. **Prepare the center.** (See page 3.)
2. **Introduce the center.** State the goal. Say: *You will use happy faces to measure the length of each pencil on the mats.*
3. **Teach the skill.** Demonstrate how to use the center with individual students or small groups.
4. **Practice the skill.** Have students use the center independently or with a partner.

Contents

Written Practice........... 100
Center Cover................ 101
Answer Key.................. 103
Center Mats......... 105, 107
Cards........................... 109

Name ______________________ Skill: Measure length in nonstandard units

Measure It

Cut out the squares with the bees at the bottom of the page.
Place bees one above the other to measure the stem of each flower.
Count the bees you used and write the number in the flower.

Measure It

Skill: Measure length in nonstandard units

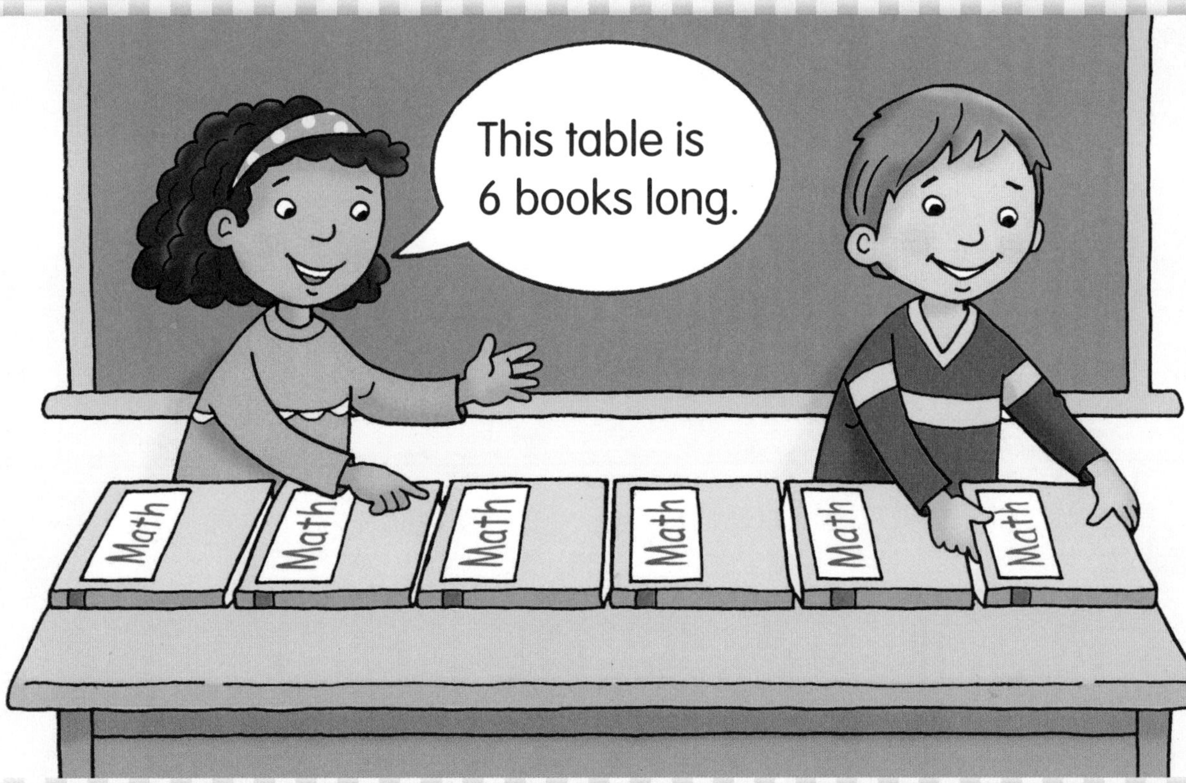

1. Lay out the mats and sort the cards into two groups: happy faces and numbers.
2. Put happy-face cards under each pencil on the mats. Lay the cards side by side, from one end of the pencil to the other.
3. Count the happy faces under the pencil.
4. Find the card with that number and put it in the colored square.
5. Do the written practice activity.

Written Practice

Measure It

Cut out the squares with the bees at the bottom of the page.
Place bees one above the other to measure the stem of each flower.
Count the bees you used and write the number in the flower.

6

5

4

3

2

(fold)

Answer Key

Measure It

Answer Key

Measure It

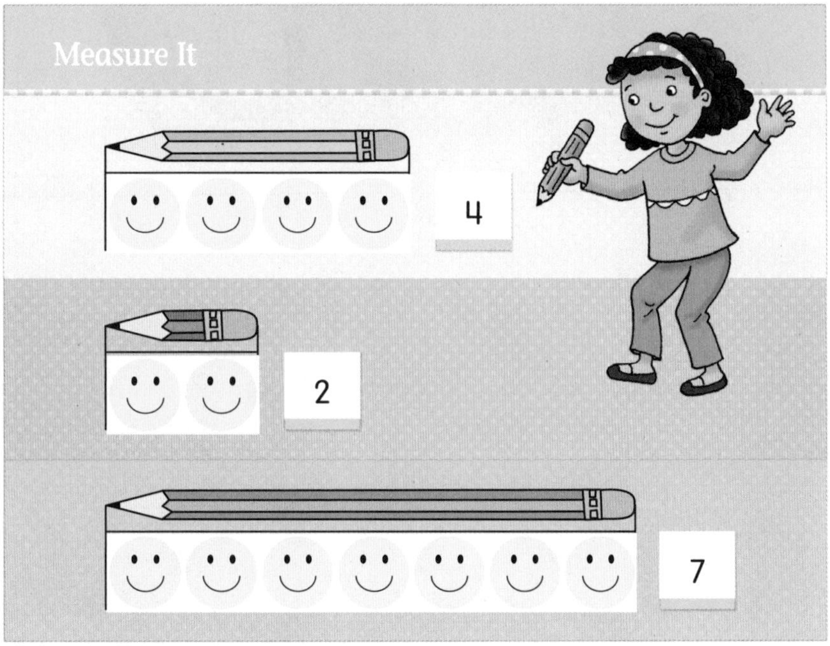

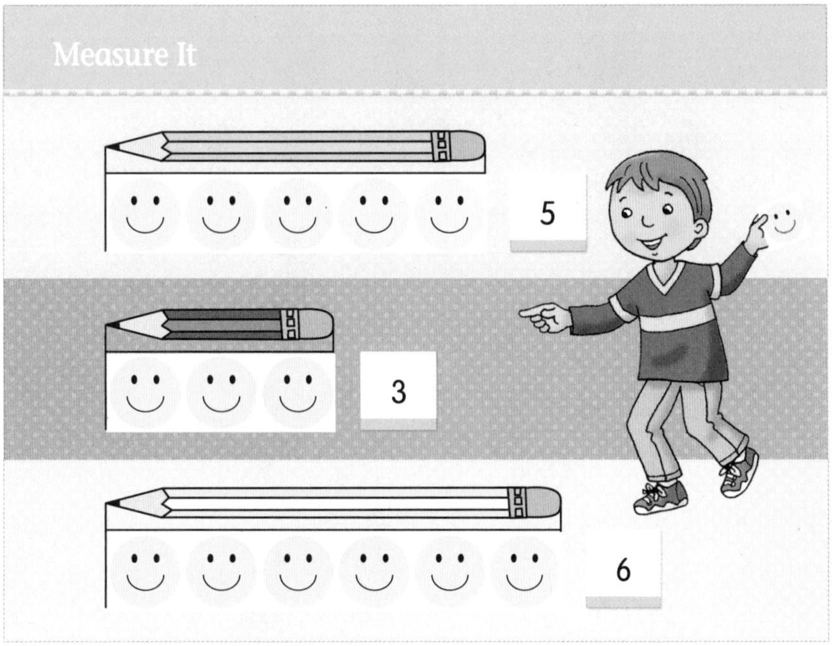

Measure It

Measure It

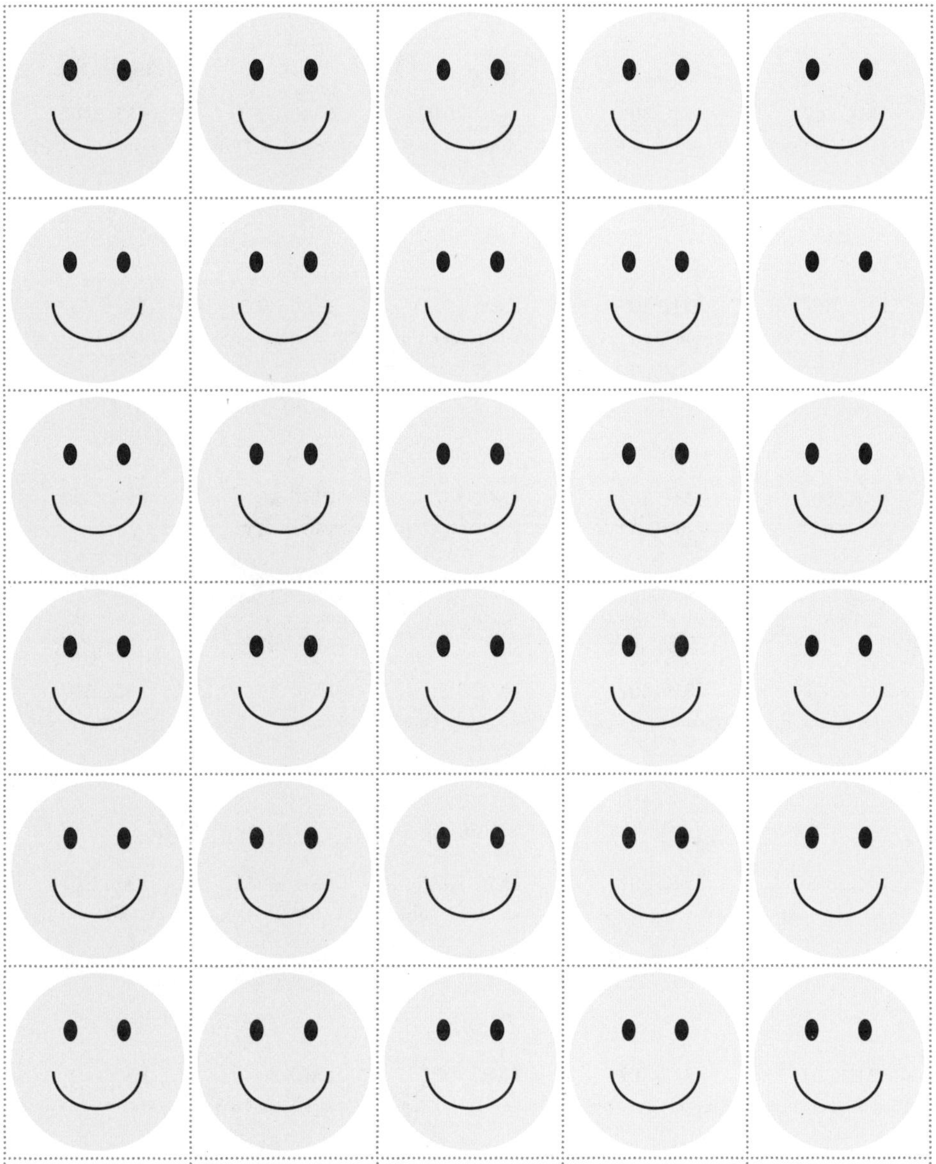

1	2	3	4	5
6	7	8	9	10

Measure It	Measure It	Measure It	Measure It	Measure It
EMC 3071	EMC 3071	EMC 3071	EMC 3071	EMC 3071
© Evan-Moor Corp.	© Evan-Moor Corp.	© Evan-Moor Corp.	© Evan-Moor Corp.	© Evan-Moor Corp.
Measure It	Measure It	Measure It	Measure It	Measure It
EMC 3071	EMC 3071	EMC 3071	EMC 3071	EMC 3071
© Evan-Moor Corp.	© Evan-Moor Corp.	© Evan-Moor Corp.	© Evan-Moor Corp.	© Evan-Moor Corp.
Measure It	Measure It	Measure It	Measure It	Measure It
EMC 3071	EMC 3071	EMC 3071	EMC 3071	EMC 3071
© Evan-Moor Corp.	© Evan-Moor Corp.	© Evan-Moor Corp.	© Evan-Moor Corp.	© Evan-Moor Corp.
Measure It	Measure It	Measure It	Measure It	Measure It
EMC 3071	EMC 3071	EMC 3071	EMC 3071	EMC 3071
© Evan-Moor Corp.	© Evan-Moor Corp.	© Evan-Moor Corp.	© Evan-Moor Corp.	© Evan-Moor Corp.
Measure It	Measure It	Measure It	Measure It	Measure It
EMC 3071	EMC 3071	EMC 3071	EMC 3071	EMC 3071
© Evan-Moor Corp.	© Evan-Moor Corp.	© Evan-Moor Corp.	© Evan-Moor Corp.	© Evan-Moor Corp.
Measure It	Measure It	Measure It	Measure It	Measure It
EMC 3071	EMC 3071	EMC 3071	EMC 3071	EMC 3071
© Evan-Moor Corp.	© Evan-Moor Corp.	© Evan-Moor Corp.	© Evan-Moor Corp.	© Evan-Moor Corp.
Measure It	Measure It	Measure It	Measure It	Measure It
EMC 3071	EMC 3071	EMC 3071	EMC 3071	EMC 3071
© Evan-Moor Corp.	© Evan-Moor Corp.	© Evan-Moor Corp.	© Evan-Moor Corp.	© Evan-Moor Corp.
Measure It	Measure It	Measure It	Measure It	Measure It
EMC 3071	EMC 3071	EMC 3071	EMC 3071	EMC 3071
© Evan-Moor Corp.	© Evan-Moor Corp.	© Evan-Moor Corp.	© Evan-Moor Corp.	© Evan-Moor Corp.

Telling Time

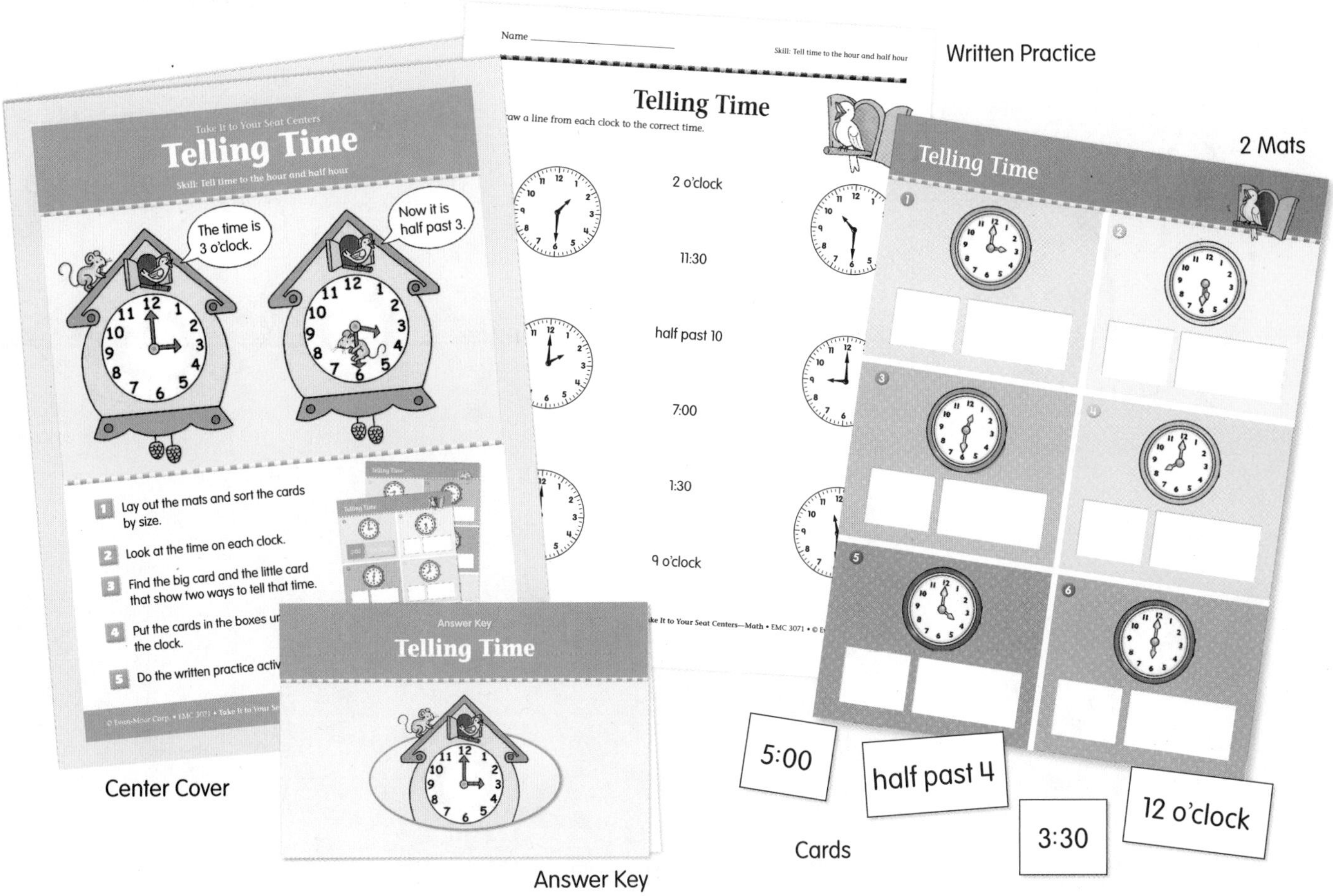

Skill: Tell time to the hour and half hour

Steps to Follow

1. **Prepare the center.** (See page 3.)
2. **Introduce the center.** State the goal. Say: *You will look at each clock on the mats and find the two cards that tell what time it is.*
3. **Teach the skill.** Demonstrate how to use the center with individual students or small groups.
4. **Practice the skill.** Have students use the center independently or with a partner.

Contents

Written Practice........... 112
Center Cover................ 113
Answer Key.................. 115
Center Mats.......... 117, 119
Cards.......................... 121

Name ____________________ Skill: Tell time to the hour and half hour

Telling Time

Draw a line from each clock to the correct time.

2 o'clock

11:30

half past 10

7:00

1:30

9 o'clock

Take It to Your Seat Centers

Telling Time

Skill: Tell time to the hour and half hour

1. Lay out the mats and sort the cards by size.
2. Look at the time on each clock.
3. Find the big card and the little card that show two ways to tell that time.
4. Put the cards in the boxes under the clock.
5. Do the written practice activity.

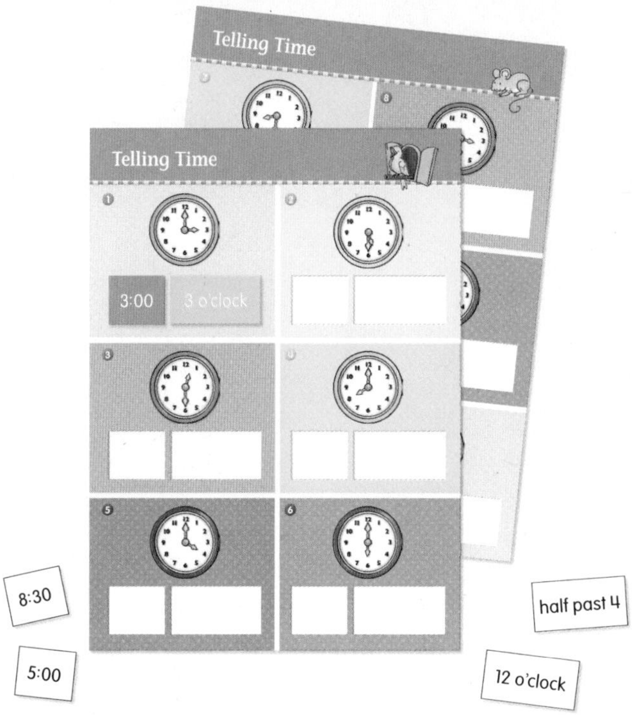

Written Practice

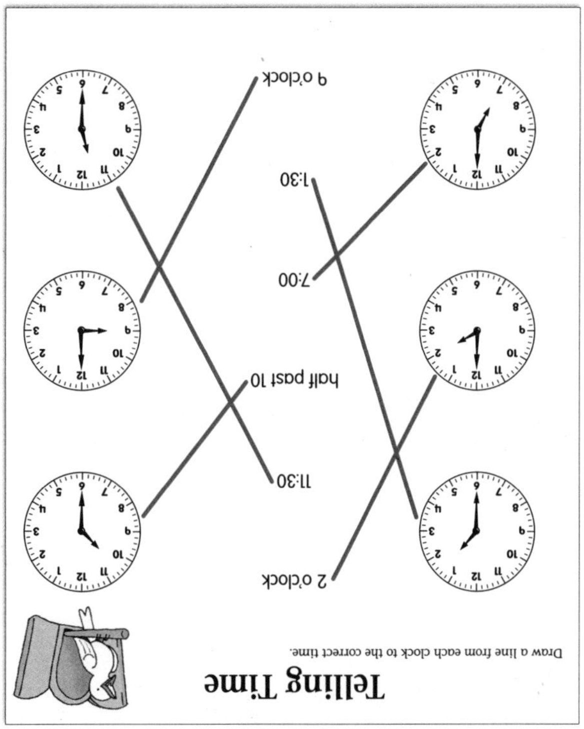

(fold)

Answer Key

Telling Time

Answer Key

Telling Time

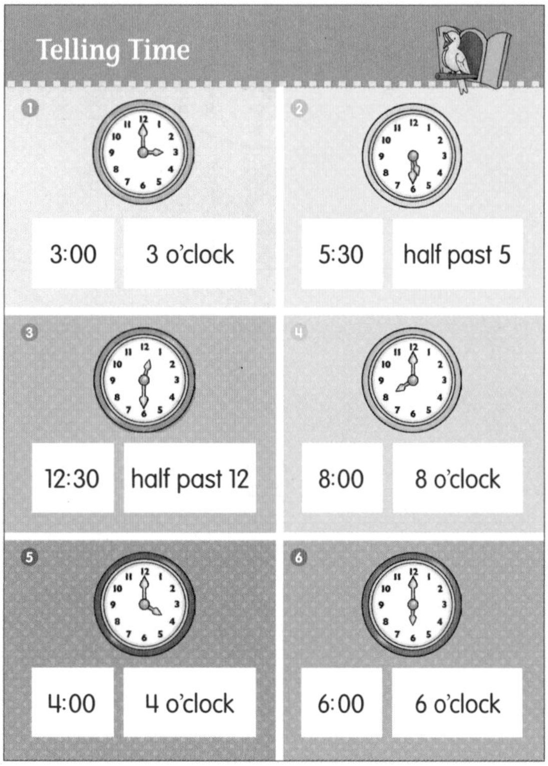

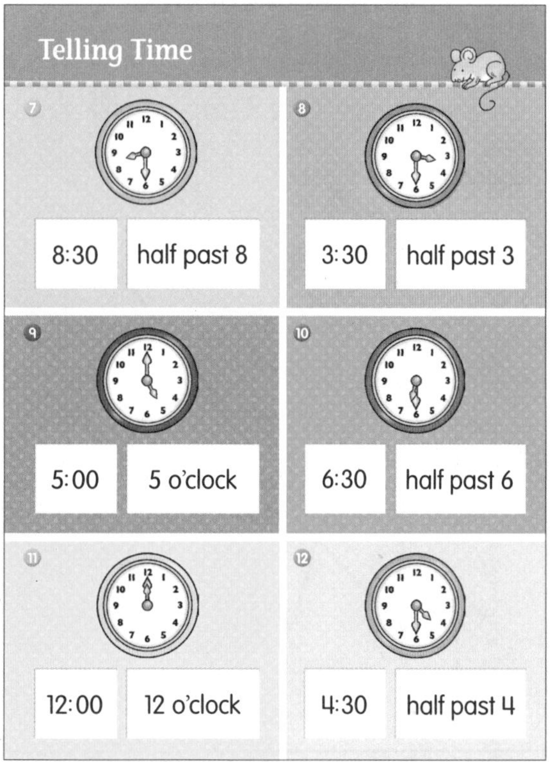

Telling Time

1

2

3

4

5

6

Telling Time

7

8

9

10

11

12

3:00	3:30
4:00	4:30
5:00	5:30
6:00	6:30
8:00	8:30
12:00	12:30

3 o'clock	half past 3
4 o'clock	half past 4
5 o'clock	half past 5
6 o'clock	half past 6
8 o'clock	half past 8
12 o'clock	half past 12

Telling Time
EMC 3071
© Evan-Moor Corp.

Telling Time
EMC 3071
© Evan-Moor Corp.

Telling Time
EMC 3071
© Evan-Moor Corp.

Telling Time
EMC 3071
© Evan-Moor Corp.

Telling Time
EMC 3071
© Evan-Moor Corp.

Telling Time
EMC 3071
© Evan-Moor Corp.

Telling Time
EMC 3071
© Evan-Moor Corp.

Telling Time
EMC 3071
© Evan-Moor Corp.

Telling Time
EMC 3071
© Evan-Moor Corp.

Telling Time
EMC 3071
© Evan-Moor Corp.

Telling Time
EMC 3071
© Evan-Moor Corp.

Telling Time
EMC 3071
© Evan-Moor Corp.

Telling Time
EMC 3071
© Evan-Moor Corp.

Telling Time
EMC 3071
© Evan-Moor Corp.

Telling Time
EMC 3071
© Evan-Moor Corp.

Telling Time
EMC 3071
© Evan-Moor Corp.

Telling Time
EMC 3071
© Evan-Moor Corp.

Telling Time
EMC 3071
© Evan-Moor Corp.

Telling Time
EMC 3071
© Evan-Moor Corp.

Telling Time
EMC 3071
© Evan-Moor Corp.

Telling Time
EMC 3071
© Evan-Moor Corp.

Telling Time
EMC 3071
© Evan-Moor Corp.

Telling Time
EMC 3071
© Evan-Moor Corp.

Telling Time
EMC 3071
© Evan-Moor Corp.

Take It to Your Seat Centers

Make a Graph

Skill: Build and read a bar graph

Steps to Follow

1. **Prepare the center.** (See page 3.)
2. **Introduce the center.** State the goal. Say: *You will make a bar graph and use it to answer questions about the data.*
3. **Teach the skill.** Demonstrate how to use the center with individual students or small groups.
4. **Practice the skill.** Have students use the center independently or with a partner.

Contents

Written Practice........... 124
Center Cover................ 125
Answer Key.................. 127
Center Mats..........129, 131
Cards.......................... 133

Name ____________________

Skill: Build and read a bar graph

Make a Graph

Read the color word. Then use that color to fill in the number of boxes that shows how many of each bird the children saw at the park.

black 						
red 						
yellow 						
blue 						
brown 						
	1	2	3	4	5	6

Use the graph to answer these questions.

How many? red birds ______ yellow birds ______ black birds ______

brown birds ______ blue birds ______

How many more yellow birds than red birds did the children see? ______

How many more brown birds than black birds did they see? ______

How many birds did they see altogether? ______

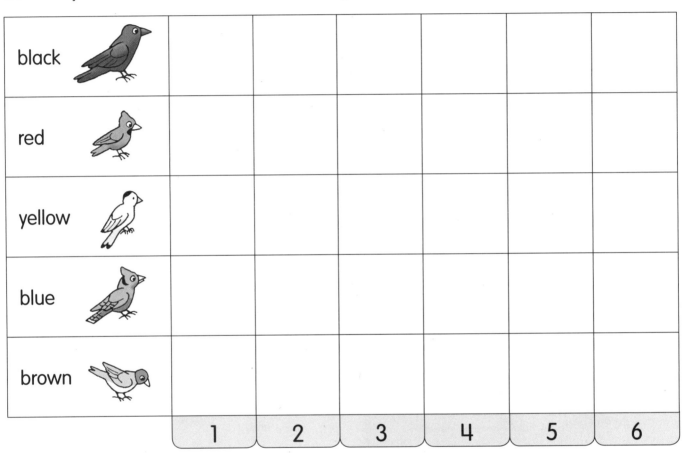

Take It to Your Seat Centers

Make a Graph

Skill: Build and read a bar graph

1. Lay out the picture of the park and the mat with the graph on it.
2. Sort the cards into groups by color.
3. Look at the picture of the park. Count the birds you see of each color.
4. Put that many colored cards in that bird's row on the graph.
5. Do the written practice activity.

Written Practice

Make a Graph

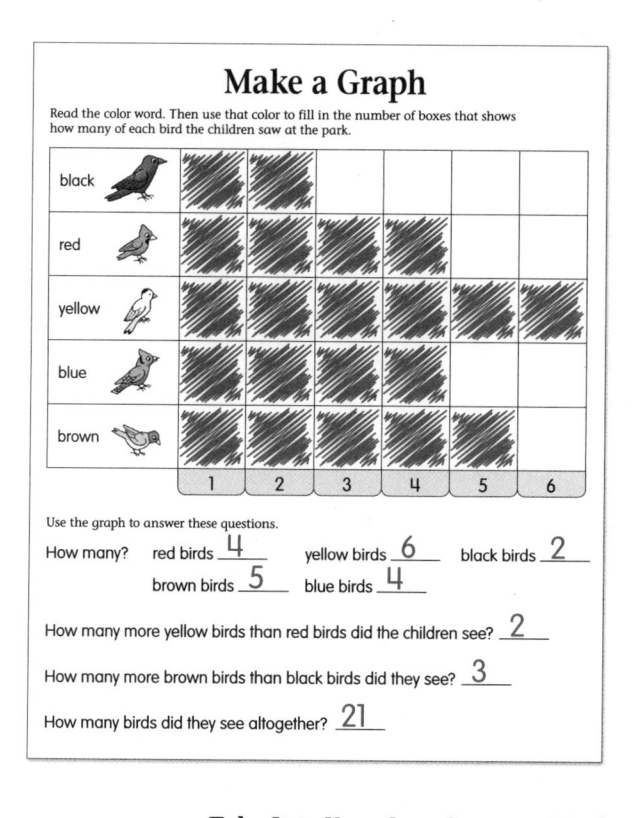

Read the color word. Then use that color to fill in the number of boxes that shows how many of each bird the children saw at the park.

	1	2	3	4	5	6
black	■	■				
red	■	■	■	■		
yellow	■	■	■	■	■	■
blue	■	■	■	■		
brown	■	■	■	■	■	

Use the graph to answer these questions.

How many? red birds 4 yellow birds 6 black birds 2

brown birds 5 blue birds 4

How many more yellow birds than red birds did the children see? 2

How many more brown birds than black birds did they see? 3

How many birds did they see altogether? 21

(fold)

Make a Graph

Answer Key

Answer Key

Make a Graph

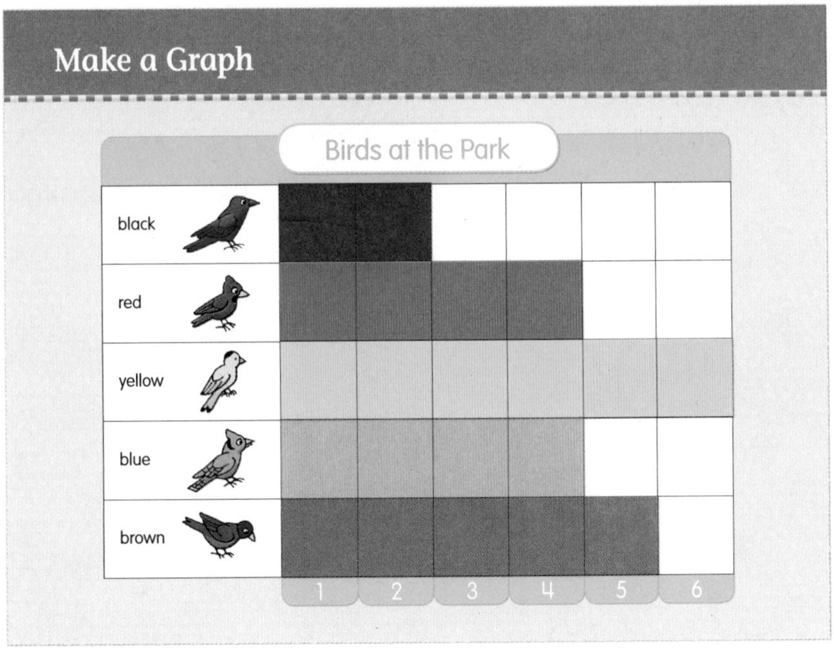

The Park

Make a Graph

Birds at the Park

black							
red							
yellow							
blue							
brown							
		1	2	3	4	5	6

Make a Graph EMC 3071 © Evan-Moor Corp.	Make a Graph EMC 3071 © Evan-Moor Corp.	Make a Graph EMC 3071 © Evan-Moor Corp.	Make a Graph EMC 3071 © Evan-Moor Corp.	Make a Graph EMC 3071 © Evan-Moor Corp.	Make a Graph EMC 3071 © Evan-Moor Corp.	Make a Graph EMC 3071 © Evan-Moor Corp.
Make a Graph EMC 3071 © Evan-Moor Corp.	Make a Graph EMC 3071 © Evan-Moor Corp.	Make a Graph EMC 3071 © Evan-Moor Corp.	Make a Graph EMC 3071 © Evan-Moor Corp.	Make a Graph EMC 3071 © Evan-Moor Corp.	Make a Graph EMC 3071 © Evan-Moor Corp.	Make a Graph EMC 3071 © Evan-Moor Corp.
Make a Graph EMC 3071 © Evan-Moor Corp.	Make a Graph EMC 3071 © Evan-Moor Corp.	Make a Graph EMC 3071 © Evan-Moor Corp.	Make a Graph EMC 3071 © Evan-Moor Corp.	Make a Graph EMC 3071 © Evan-Moor Corp.	Make a Graph EMC 3071 © Evan-Moor Corp.	Make a Graph EMC 3071 © Evan-Moor Corp.
Make a Graph EMC 3071 © Evan-Moor Corp.	Make a Graph EMC 3071 © Evan-Moor Corp.	Make a Graph EMC 3071 © Evan-Moor Corp.	Make a Graph EMC 3071 © Evan-Moor Corp.	Make a Graph EMC 3071 © Evan-Moor Corp.	Make a Graph EMC 3071 © Evan-Moor Corp.	Make a Graph EMC 3071 © Evan-Moor Corp.
Make a Graph EMC 3071 © Evan-Moor Corp.	Make a Graph EMC 3071 © Evan-Moor Corp.	Make a Graph EMC 3071 © Evan-Moor Corp.	Make a Graph EMC 3071 © Evan-Moor Corp.	Make a Graph EMC 3071 © Evan-Moor Corp.	Make a Graph EMC 3071 © Evan-Moor Corp.	Make a Graph EMC 3071 © Evan-Moor Corp.
Make a Graph EMC 3071 © Evan-Moor Corp.	Make a Graph EMC 3071 © Evan-Moor Corp.	Make a Graph EMC 3071 © Evan-Moor Corp.	Make a Graph EMC 3071 © Evan-Moor Corp.	Make a Graph EMC 3071 © Evan-Moor Corp.	Make a Graph EMC 3071 © Evan-Moor Corp.	Make a Graph EMC 3071 © Evan-Moor Corp.

What Shape Is It?

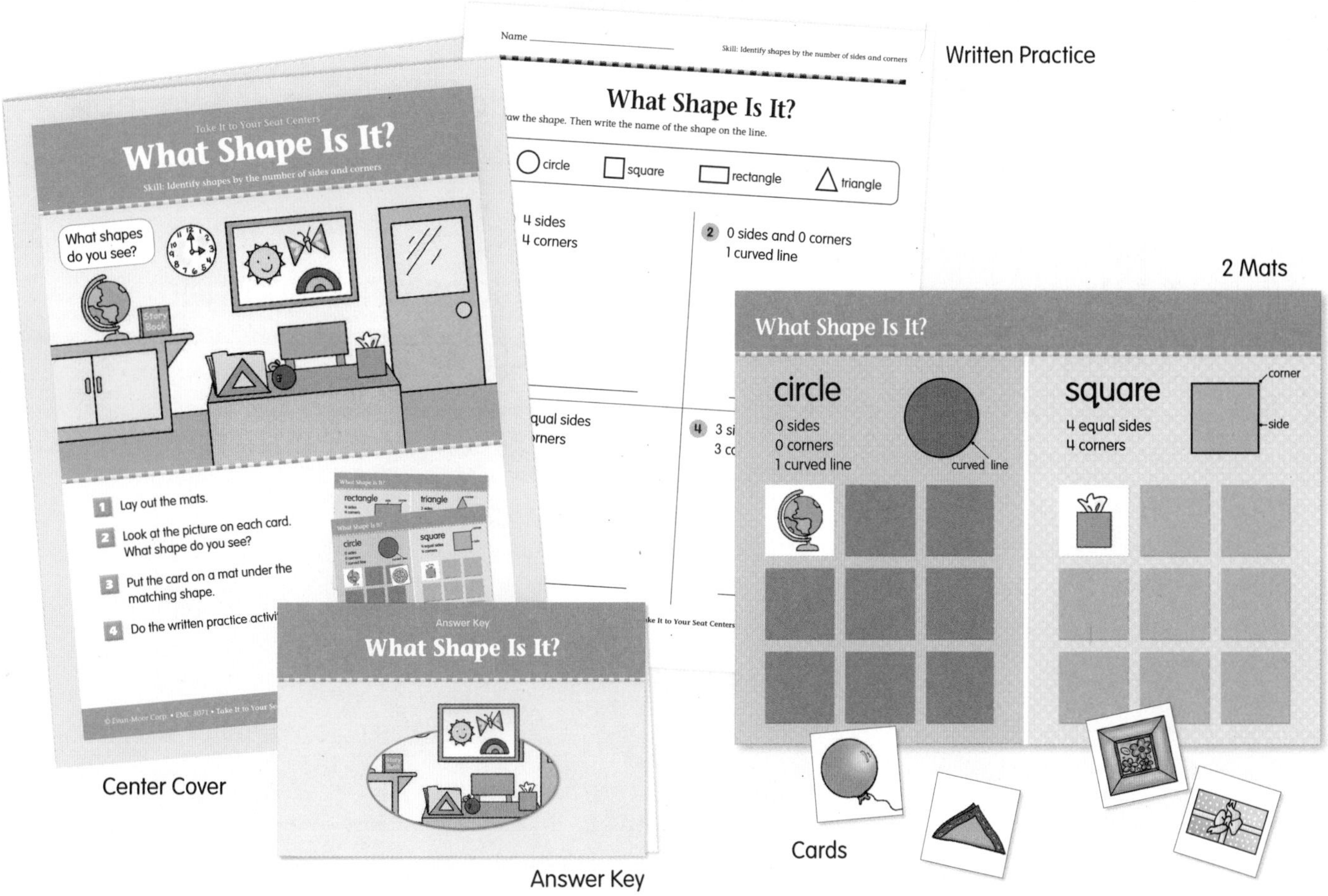

Skill: Identify shapes by the number of sides and corners

Steps to Follow

1. **Prepare the center.** (See page 3.)
2. **Introduce the center.** State the goal. Say: *You will put each card on a mat under the shape of the object that you see on the card.*
3. **Teach the skill.** Demonstrate how to use the center with individual students or small groups.
4. **Practice the skill.** Have students use the center independently or with a partner.

Contents

Written Practice........... 136
Center Cover................ 137
Answer Key.................. 139
Center Mats.......... 141, 143
Cards........................... 145

Name ______________________________

Skill: Identify shapes by the number of sides and corners

What Shape Is It?

Draw the shape. Then write the name of the shape on the line.

circle square rectangle triangle

1 4 sides
4 corners

____

2 0 sides and 0 corners
1 curved line

____

3 4 equal sides
4 corners

____

4 3 sides
3 corners

____

What Shape Is It?

Skill: Identify shapes by the number of sides and corners

1. Lay out the mats.
2. Look at the picture on each card. What shape do you see?
3. Put the card on a mat under the matching shape.
4. Do the written practice activity.

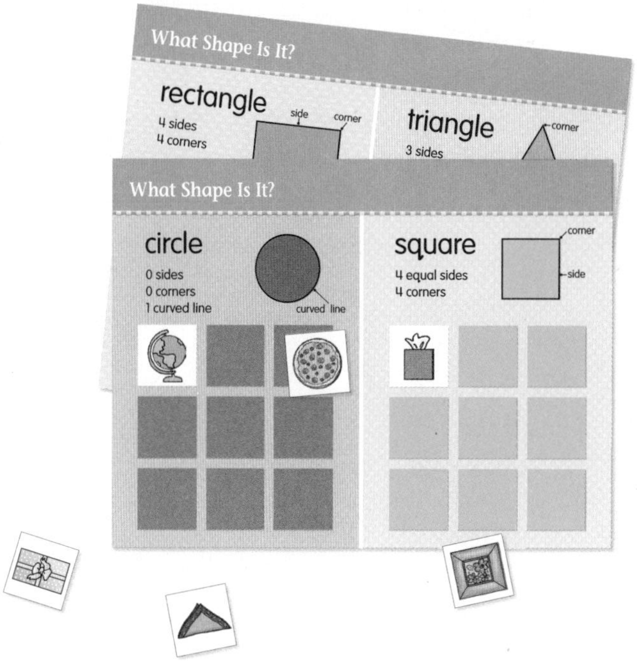

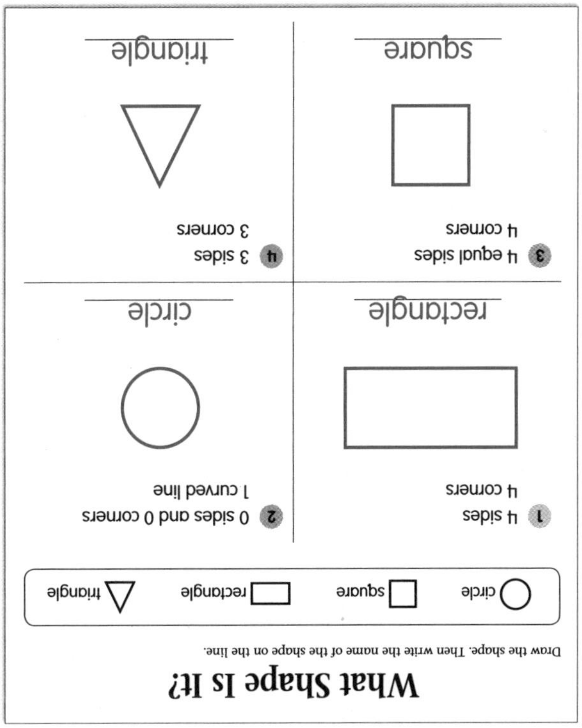

What Shape Is It?

Draw the shape. Then write the name of the shape on the line.

circle · square · rectangle · triangle

1. 4 sides
   4 corners
   rectangle
2. 0 sides and 0 corners
   1 curved line
   circle
3. 4 equal sides
   4 corners
   square
4. 3 sides
   3 corners
   triangle

Written Practice

(fold)

Answer Key

What Shape Is It?

Answer Key

What Shape Is It?

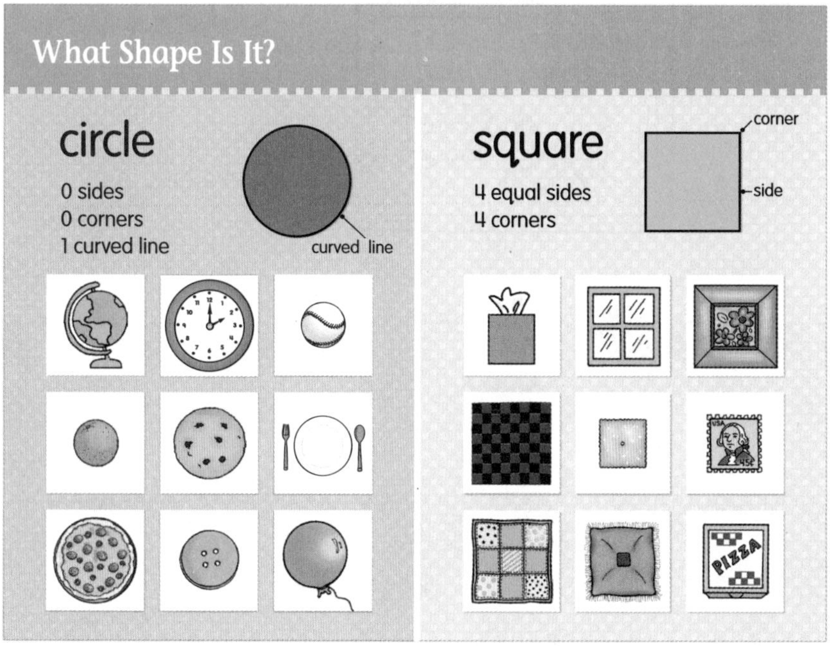

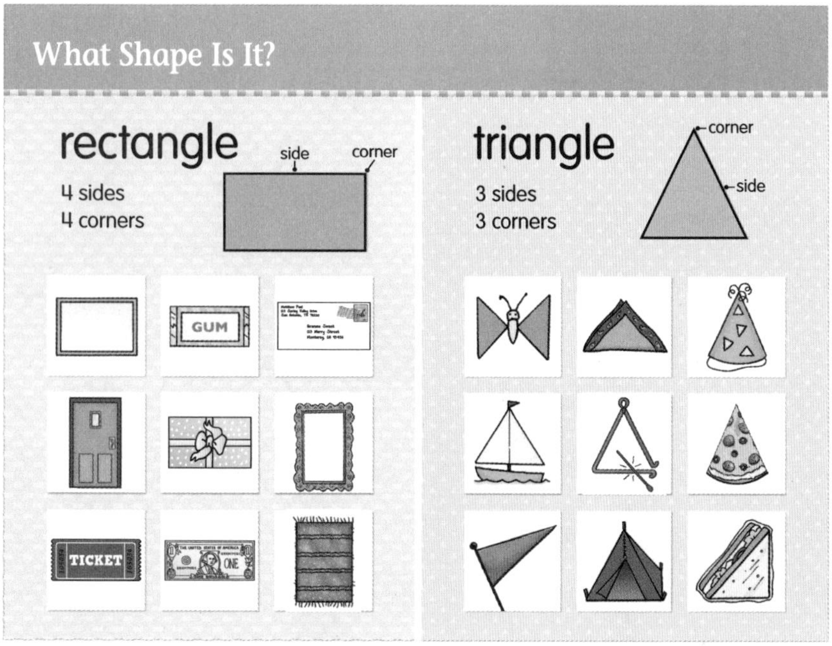

What Shape Is It?

circle

0 sides
0 corners
1 curved line

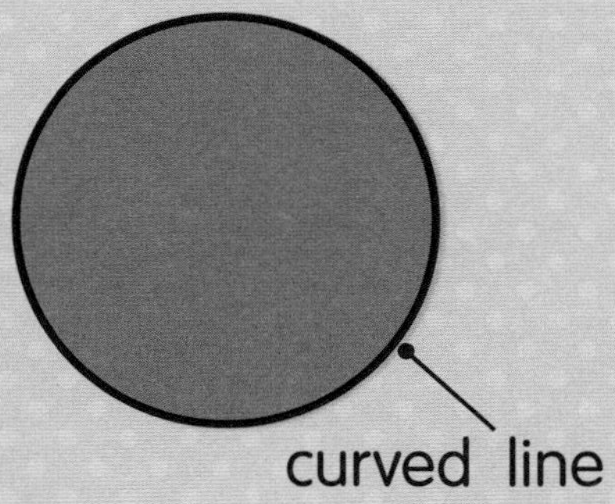

square

4 equal sides
4 corners

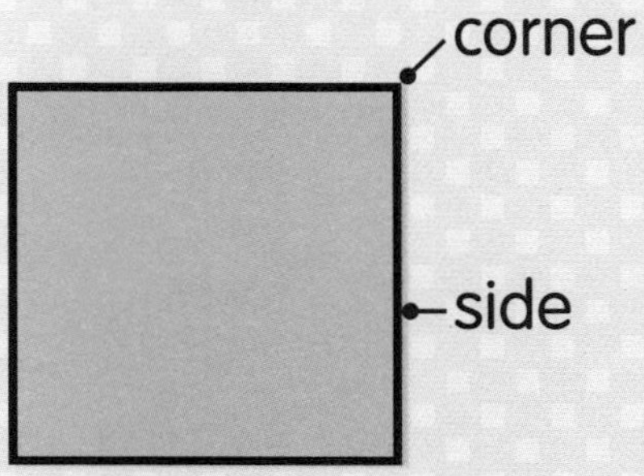

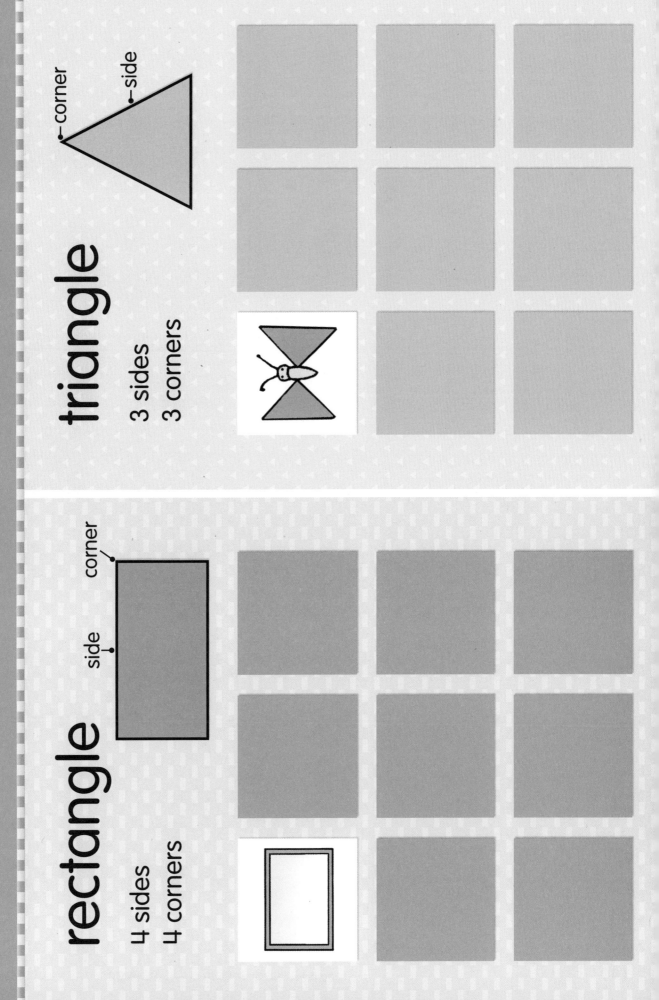

What Shape Is It?

rectangle

4 sides
4 corners

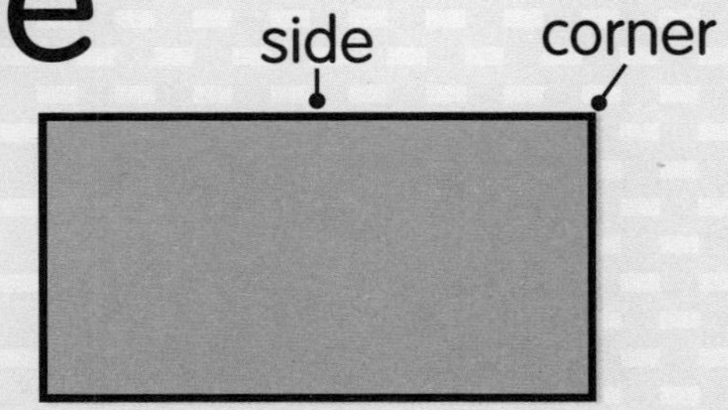

triangle

3 sides
3 corners

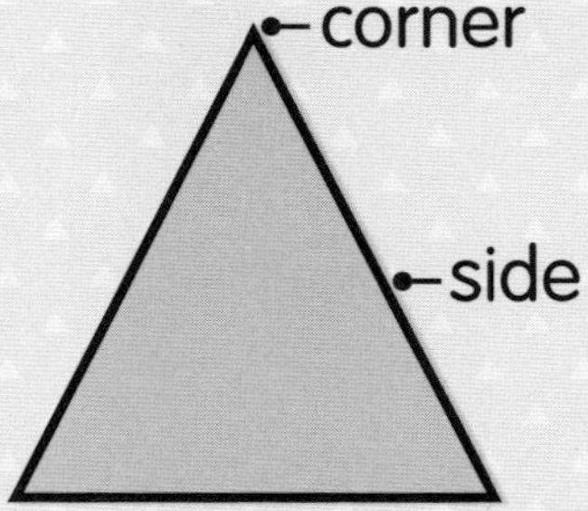

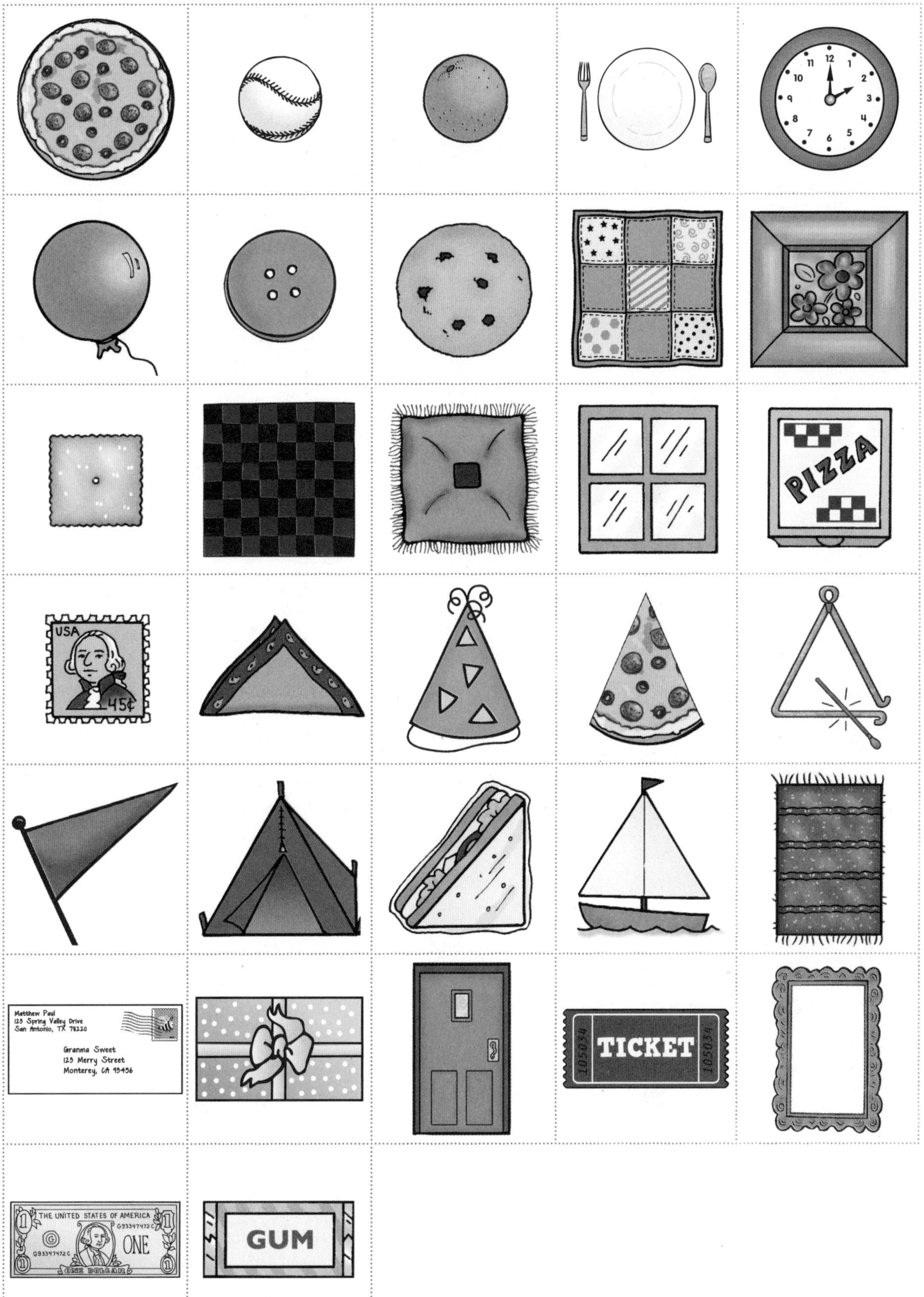
PIZZA
USA
45¢
Matthew Paul
123 Spring Valley Drive
San Antonio, TX 78220
Granma Sweet
123 Merry Street
Monterey, CA 93456
TICKET
105034
THE UNITED STATES OF AMERICA
ONE
ONE DOLLAR
GUM

What Shape Is It?
EMC 3071
© Evan-Moor Corp.

What Shape Is It?
EMC 3071
© Evan-Moor Corp.

What Shape Is It?
EMC 3071
© Evan-Moor Corp.

What Shape Is It?
EMC 3071
© Evan-Moor Corp.

What Shape Is It?
EMC 3071
© Evan-Moor Corp.

What Shape Is It?
EMC 3071
© Evan-Moor Corp.

What Shape Is It?
EMC 3071
© Evan-Moor Corp.

What Shape Is It?
EMC 3071
© Evan-Moor Corp.

What Shape Is It?
EMC 3071
© Evan-Moor Corp.

What Shape Is It?
EMC 3071
© Evan-Moor Corp.

What Shape Is It?
EMC 3071
© Evan-Moor Corp.

What Shape Is It?
EMC 3071
© Evan-Moor Corp.

What Shape Is It?
EMC 3071
© Evan-Moor Corp.

What Shape Is It?
EMC 3071
© Evan-Moor Corp.

What Shape Is It?
EMC 3071
© Evan-Moor Corp.

What Shape Is It?
EMC 3071
© Evan-Moor Corp.

What Shape Is It?
EMC 3071
© Evan-Moor Corp.

What Shape Is It?
EMC 3071
© Evan-Moor Corp.

What Shape Is It?
EMC 3071
© Evan-Moor Corp.

What Shape Is It?
EMC 3071
© Evan-Moor Corp.

What Shape Is It?
EMC 3071
© Evan-Moor Corp.

What Shape Is It?
EMC 3071
© Evan-Moor Corp.

What Shape Is It?
EMC 3071
© Evan-Moor Corp.

What Shape Is It?
EMC 3071
© Evan-Moor Corp.

What Shape Is It?
EMC 3071
© Evan-Moor Corp.

What Shape Is It?
EMC 3071
© Evan-Moor Corp.

What Shape Is It?
EMC 3071
© Evan-Moor Corp.

What Shape Is It?
EMC 3071
© Evan-Moor Corp.

What Shape Is It?
EMC 3071
© Evan-Moor Corp.

What Shape Is It?
EMC 3071
© Evan-Moor Corp.

What Shape Is It?
EMC 3071
© Evan-Moor Corp.

What Shape Is It?
EMC 3071
© Evan-Moor Corp.

Fractional Parts

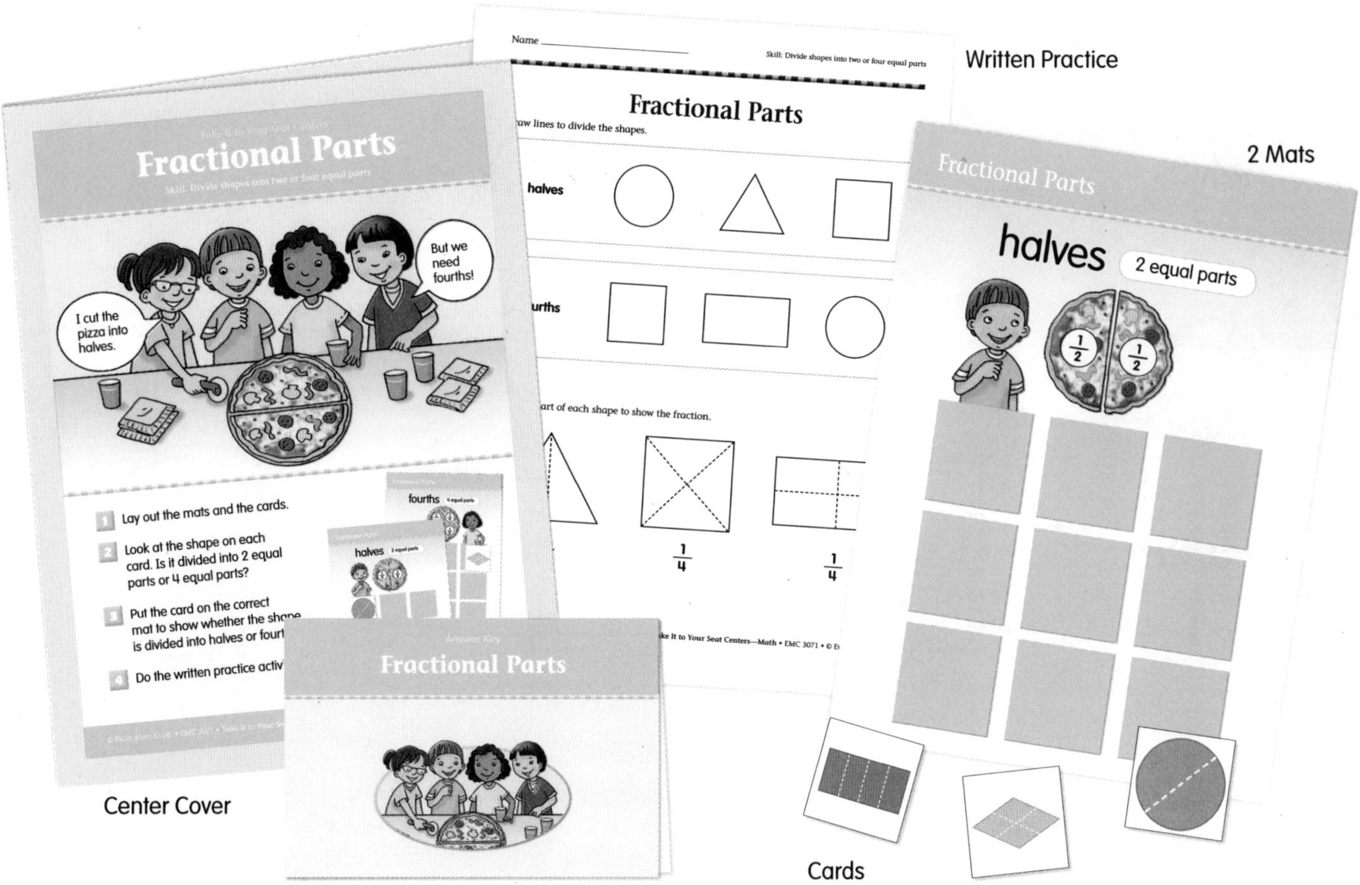

Answer Key

Skill: Divide shapes into two or four equal parts

Steps to Follow

1. **Prepare the center.** (See page 3.)
2. **Introduce the center.** State the goal. Say: *You will put each card on the correct mat to show whether the shape on the card is divided into halves or fourths.*
3. **Teach the skill.** Demonstrate how to use the center with individual students or small groups.
4. **Practice the skill.** Have students use the center independently or with a partner.

Contents

Written Practice........... 148
Center Cover................ 149
Answer Key.................. 151
Center Mats 153, 155
Cards 157, 159

Fractional Parts

Draw lines to divide the shapes.

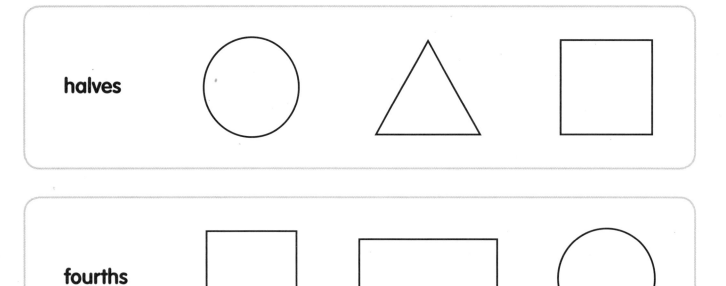

halves

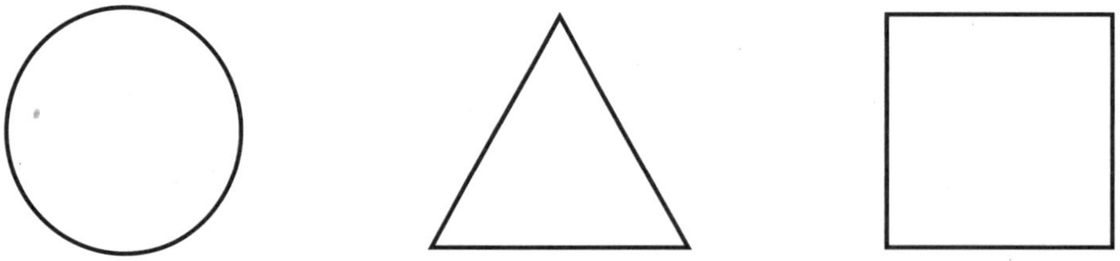

fourths

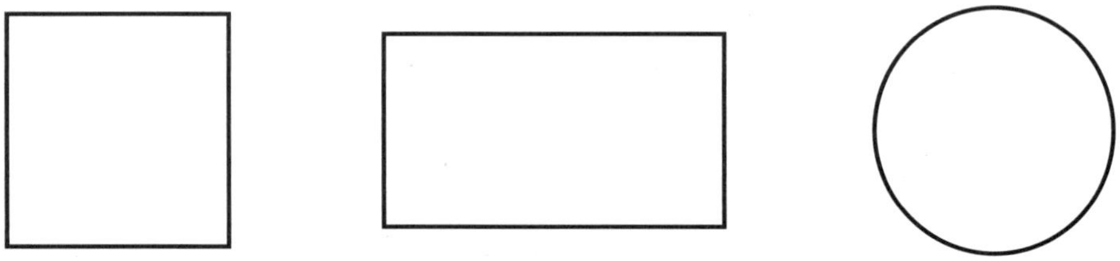

Color one part of each shape to show the fraction.

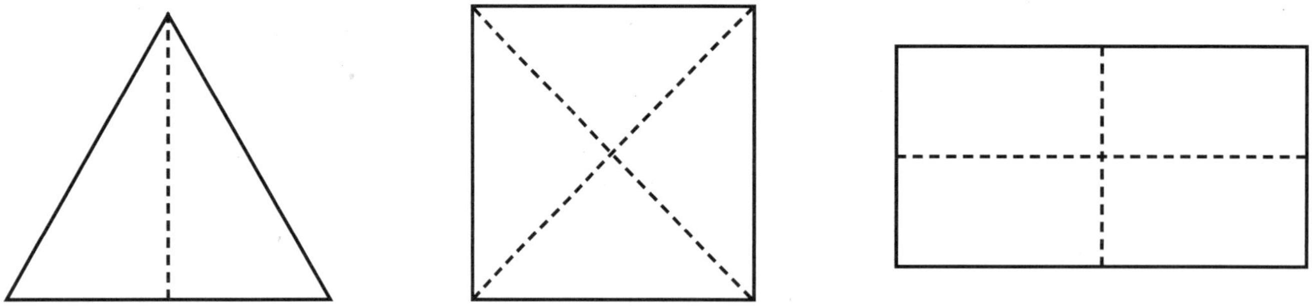

$\frac{1}{2}$ $\frac{1}{4}$ $\frac{1}{4}$

Fractional Parts

Skill: Divide shapes into two or four equal parts

I cut the pizza into halves.
But we need fourths!

1. Lay out the mats and the cards.
2. Look at the shape on each card. Is it divided into 2 equal parts or 4 equal parts?
3. Put the card on the correct mat to show whether the shape is divided into halves or fourths.
4. Do the written practice activity.

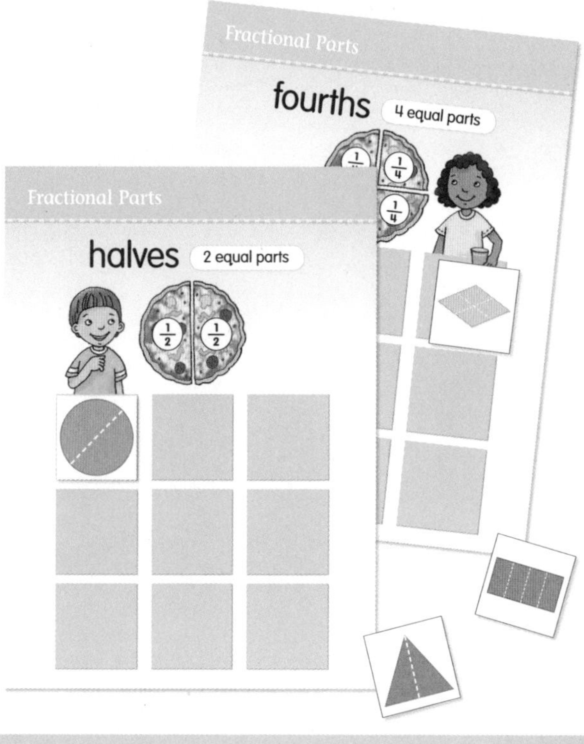
Fractional Parts
fourths
4 equal parts
Fractional Parts
halves
2 equal parts

Written Practice

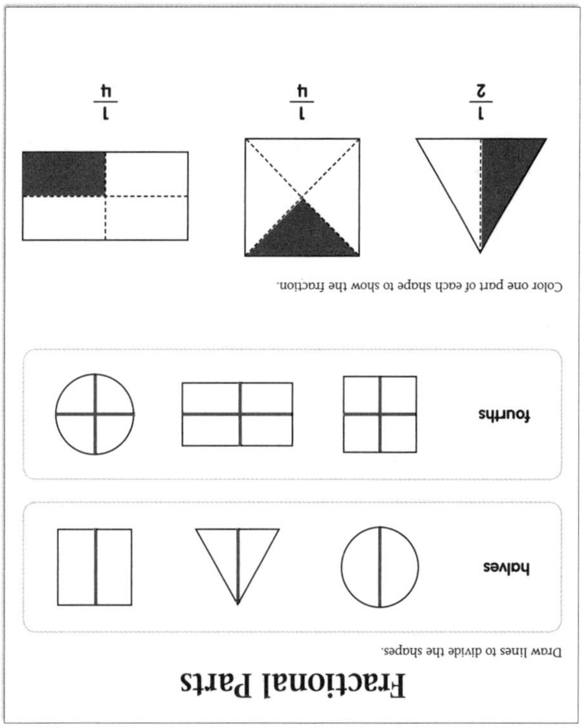

Fractional Parts
Draw lines to divide the shapes.
halves
fourths
Color one part of each shape to show the fraction.
1/2
1/4
1/4

(fold)

Answer Key

Fractional Parts

Answer Key

Fractional Parts

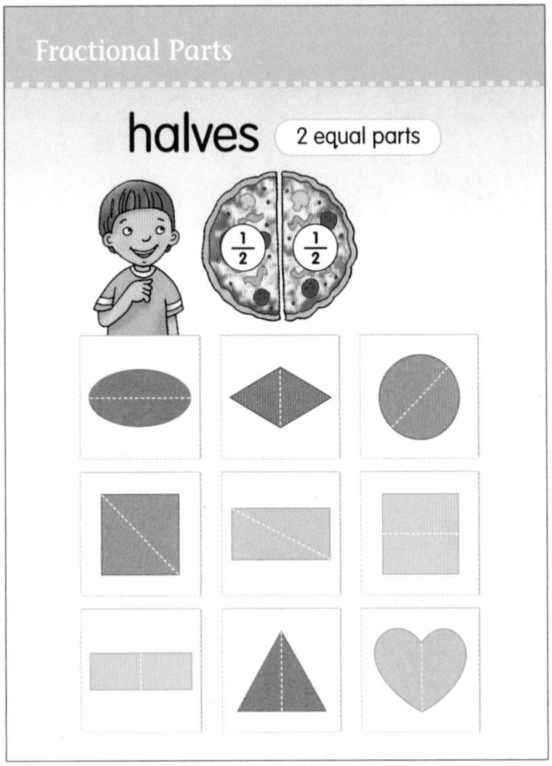

halves

2 equal parts

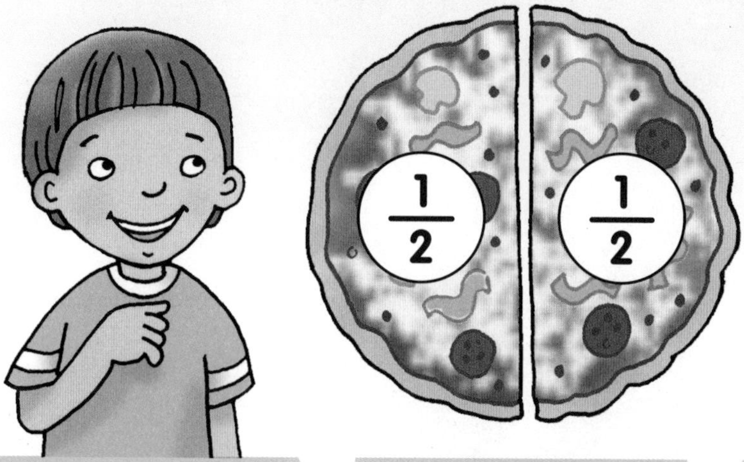

fourths

4 equal parts

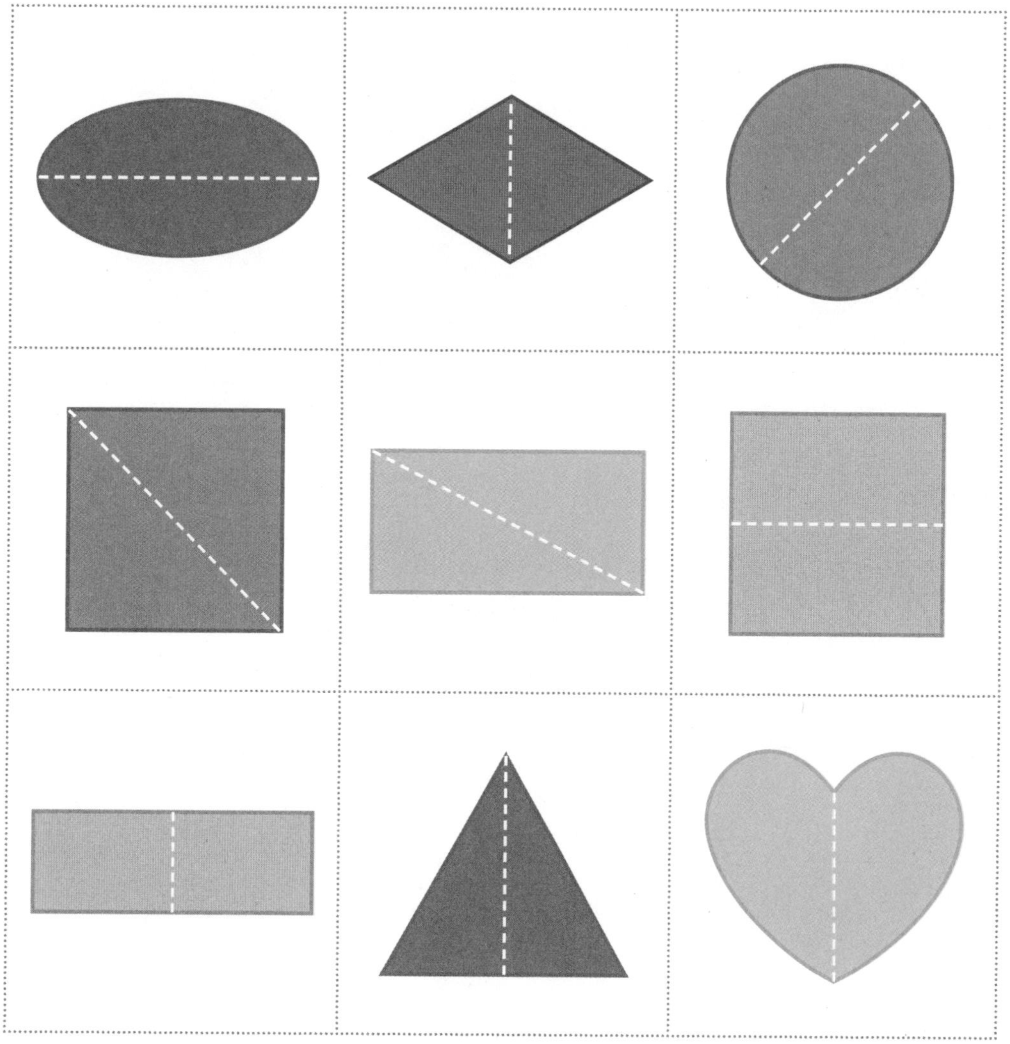

Fractional Parts

EMC 3071
© Evan-Moor Corp.

Fractional Parts

EMC 3071
© Evan-Moor Corp.

Fractional Parts

EMC 3071
© Evan-Moor Corp.

Fractional Parts

EMC 3071
© Evan-Moor Corp.

Fractional Parts

EMC 3071
© Evan-Moor Corp.

Fractional Parts

EMC 3071
© Evan-Moor Corp.

Fractional Parts

EMC 3071
© Evan-Moor Corp.

Fractional Parts

EMC 3071
© Evan-Moor Corp.

Fractional Parts

EMC 3071
© Evan-Moor Corp.

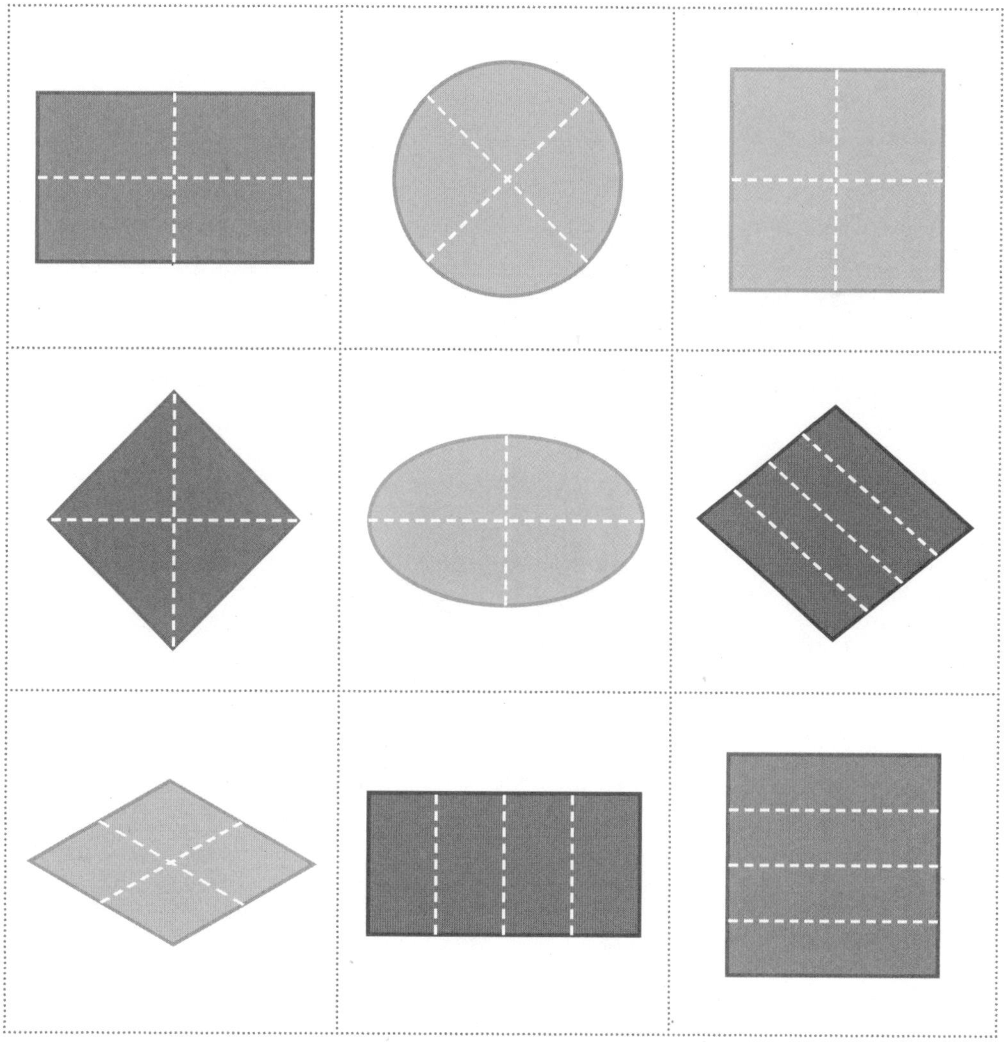

Fractional Parts

EMC 3071
© Evan-Moor Corp.

Fractional Parts

EMC 3071
© Evan-Moor Corp.

Fractional Parts

EMC 3071
© Evan-Moor Corp.

Fractional Parts

EMC 3071
© Evan-Moor Corp.

Fractional Parts

EMC 3071
© Evan-Moor Corp.

Fractional Parts

EMC 3071
© Evan-Moor Corp.

Fractional Parts

EMC 3071
© Evan-Moor Corp.

Fractional Parts

EMC 3071
© Evan-Moor Corp.

Fractional Parts

EMC 3071
© Evan-Moor Corp.